TEN ESSAYS
ON PATRICK WHITE

Selected from *Southerly* (1964-67)

G. A. WILKES

ANGUS AND ROBERTSON

First published in 1970 by
ANGUS AND ROBERTSON LTD
221 George Street, Sydney
54 Bartholomew Close, London
107 Elizabeth Street, Melbourne
89 Anson Road, Singapore

© *English Association 1970*

This book is copyright.
Apart from any fair dealing for the purposes of
private study, research, criticism or review,
as permitted under the Copyright Act,
no part may be reproduced by any process
without written permission.
Inquiries should be addressed to the publishers.

National Library of Australia card number and
ISBN 0 207 12015 3

Registered in Australia for transmission by post as a book
PRINTED IN AUSTRALIA BY HALSTEAD PRESS, SYDNEY

Preface

THE initial prompting for this collection came from continued requests for the Patrick White special number of *Southerly* (Number One of 1965), which had gone out of print. The discussion begun in that number had meanwhile continued in later issues of the journal, stimulated in turn by the publication of White's *Four Plays* (1965) and of *The Solid Mandala* (1966). By extending the scope of the selection, it therefore seemed possible to offer a more comprehensive study of Patrick White as novelist, playwright and short-story writer than was elsewhere available between two covers.

The article by Dr J. F. Burrows on "The Short Stories of Patrick White" first appeared in *Southerly* in 1964, before White had assembled his short stories in the volume *The Burnt Ones*. It is accordingly published now in a revised form. Except for changes of detail, the other articles are published as they first appeared.

G. A. WILKES

Sydney,
November 1969.

Contents

I NOVELS

Odyssey of a Spinster: A Study of *The Aunt's Story*
    THELMA HERRING   3

Patrick White's *The Tree of Man* G. A. WILKES   21

The Gothic Splendours: Patrick White's *Voss*
    JAMES McAULEY   34

Archetypes and Stereotypes: *Riders in the Chariot*
    J. F. BURROWS   47

Self and Shadow: The Quest for Totality in *The Solid Mandala* THELMA HERRING   72

II SOME RECONSIDERATIONS

"Jardin Exotique": The Central Phase of *The Aunt's Story* J. F. BURROWS   85

Visions of the Mandala in *The Tree of Man*
    A. P. RIEMER   109

A Reading of Patrick White's *Voss* G. A. WILKES   127

III PLAYS AND SHORT STORIES

Maenads and Goat-Song: The Plays of Patrick White
    THELMA HERRING   147

The Short Stories of Patrick White J. F. BURROWS   163

I NOVELS

Odyssey of a Spinster: A Study of *The Aunt's Story*

THELMA HERRING

"But old Mrs Goodman did die at last." The first eight words of a novel have seldom told so much as the arresting opening of *The Aunt's Story*. Introducing the name of the woman whose domination of her family determines much that happens in the early chapters, it establishes the fact of her death before the story moves back into the past: the unconventional conjunction at the beginning, giving a sense of continuity, plunges us into the flux of events, and, complemented by "old" and "at last", hints at the long period of frustration for at any rate one survivor which has preceded. It is a warning that we are entering upon a novel in which style is important, in which we need to pay more than the usual amount of attention to words.

As Australia's most experimental novelist Patrick White owes nothing to local literary tradition. His affinity is with those who have tried to extend the frontiers of the novel in the direction of poetry. One imagines he would assent to the view expressed by Virginia Woolf in 1927 that the future of the novel lay in a compromise between prose fiction and poetry, the taking on by fiction of "something of the exaltation of poetry, but much of the ordinariness of prose".[1] From the beginning this trend has been discernible in his work.

The Aunt's Story (1948), the third of White's novels to be published, is the first which fully reveals him as an artist of powerful and original vision. Although it may have been overshadowed in critical attention and popular esteem by the three novels of larger scope written since his return to Aus-

[1] "The Narrow Bridge of Art", in *Granite and Rainbow*, p. 18.

tralia, on its smaller scale it sets out to do something no less difficult and, I would argue, achieves its end more successfully. True, it has not the tortured intensity of *Voss*, nothing perhaps quite so continuously impressive and moving as the account of Himmelfarb's life in Europe in *Riders in the Chariot*: but neither has it the disconcerting inequalities of these novels and *The Tree of Man*.

Tentative though they are in many ways, White's first two novels show him already grappling with themes which were to engage him at a deeper level in *The Aunt's Story*, and seeking to adapt the techniques of Joyce and Virginia Woolf (not yet fully assimilated) to present what is to him the basic human problem: "the ultimate separateness of soul".[2] *Happy Valley* (1939), though it is his least characteristic novel, is typical in concerning itself with "a world of allegory, of which the dominating motif was pain" (p. 77), and the epigraph from Mahatma Gandhi on the law of suffering, which ends: "the purer the suffering, the greater is the progress", is even more applicable to some of the later books, including *The Aunt's Story*, than to *Happy Valley* itself, which does not explore the theme fully. It anticipates *The Aunt's Story* in showing that the sensitive human being can hope for happiness only in rare moments of illumination: through art, as when Oliver Halliday listens to Bach played in a French church; through the beauty of some object such as the shell which Rodney gives Margaret; or through a momentary recognition of affinity with another human being, as when the two lonely children exchange glances in the schoolroom. Only insensitive characters get what they want—and it is doubtful whether it is worth having. Hilda Halliday gets her dreary security by hanging on to a husband who doesn't want her; Sidney Furlow perjures herself in order to blackmail Hagan into marrying her—a very poor bargain; Amy Quong, one of whose three passions is for possession, after causing the deaths of both Vic and Ernest Moriarty by her anonymous letter, acquires Vic's lustre bowl which she has coveted.

[2] *The Living and the Dead*, p. 136. References are to the following editions of the early novels: *Happy Valley* (Harrap, 1939); *The Living and the Dead* (Eyre and Spottiswoode, 1962); *The Aunt's Story* (Eyre and Spottiswoode, 1958).

The character who emerges as the most highly developed human being is the outsider Margaret Quong, half-Chinese, half-Australian, who at the age of thirteen accepts the loneliness of her destiny with a silent, touching dignity and fortitude, having learnt to expect nothing from others and to endure without useless protest.

Belief in the law of learning through suffering goes back at least to Aeschylus,[3] and several references show that Greek tragedy was indeed in White's thoughts.[4] The most substantial recalls it, however, only to draw a bitter contrast: "There is something relentless about the hatred induced by human contacts in a small town. At times it seems to have a kind of superhuman organization, like the passions in a Greek tragedy, but there is seldom any nobility about the passions of a small town . . ." (p. 191). Hatred for the meanness of the herd, its incapacity to suffer and to learn, balances White's compassion for the fear and pain and loneliness of the individual; *Happy Valley* is an early study of the ignoble small community of which Sarsaparilla later becomes the symbol.

But, although the point of view is characteristic, there is something unsatisfactory about the presentation of the theme. Despite various references to the search for significance, a design, in what happens, the design seems to be imposed by the author rather than discovered. The plot is very carefully patterned so that the violent climax of the story of the Moriartys provides the resolution of the other main entanglements: but one is convinced neither of the inevitability of Oliver's renunciation of Alys (he speaks of not willingly destroying, but takes no account of the probable destruction of *her* happiness), nor of the reality of the progress to which their suffering has led. Too little has been seen of Oliver and Alys *together* for us properly to judge the value of their experience, and the final impression is that they are too negative and ineffectual to make much spiritual progress.

The Living and the Dead (1941) is distinguished from White's other work by its setting, the London of the brittle

---

[3] Cf. *Agamemnon*, p. 173ff.
[4] Cf. ". . . the old woman. [the midwife], standing there as leisurely as a chorus from Euripides" (p. 14); Mrs Furlow announcing Moriarty's death "with the clarity of a Greek messenger" (p. 284).

1920s and bewildered 1930s: and far from justifying the glib assumption that as an expatriate he cannot possibly write as well about another country as about Australia, it seems to me rather to support Jack Lindsay's view that "[White's] roots lie in English culture and society".[5] It is arguable that he understands (though he may dislike them equally) Bayswater or Pimlico as a social milieu much better than Sarsaparilla; and certainly as a *place* London is much more vividly realized (and I don't refer merely to the accumulation of physical details) than, say, the Durilgai of *The Tree of Man*. The limitations of *The Living and the Dead* are not due to the choice of an English setting, but are the natural limitations of a young novelist still struggling towards maturity as an artist.

The atmosphere of this novel is one of decay, aridity, nullity, death: and the sense of stifling enclosure is intensified by the imagery—the recurring cocoon metaphor and such phrases as "an eiderdown of sleep", "the anaesthesia of snow", "the grey pall of words". London is the brown sad city of *The Waste Land*, to which spring brings no ecstasy. Even music, usually a source of beauty in White's novels, is part of the decadence: "the spun caramel of violins, a drawn-out Massenet", "a rheumaticky *pizzicato* that was Grieg" in a Lyons' Corner House. It does not need the repetition of the phrase "the marble wasteland" to recall the world of Eliot's early poems: and it is difficult not to attach significance to the choice of a name for the hero. Elyot Standish (a forerunner of the Poet in *The Ham Funeral*) is a younger Prufrock, always standing on the shore looking on, afraid of getting his feet wet, afraid of being alive.

It is through the experience of Elyot that White endeavours to work out his theme of the opposition between the spiritually dead and those who are truly alive, using several times the metaphor (also used by Virginia Woolf) of the envelope enclosing each personality, ensuring its separateness. Elyot in his fear of involving himself cherishes separateness till he perceives that he must make the crucial choice, which is complicated by the fate of the "living" char-

[5] "The Alienated Australian Intellectual", *Meanjin Quarterly*, XXII (1963), p. 58.

acters, his sister Eden and Joe Barnett, who choose spiritual "life" at the cost of death in the Spanish Civil War: but it may be objected that in preferring to "the protest of self-destruction" "an intenser form of living" (p. 331) he reaches a very vague solution.

It is misleading to say as Marjorie Barnard does that the novel "ends where it began".[6] True, the *story* returns to its beginning after showing in retrospect (like the first part of *The Aunt's Story*) the events which have culminated, just before the novel opens, in the death of the protagonist's mother. This is emphasized by the repetition at the beginning of the final chapter of the paragraph at the end of the first in which Elyot in the drawing-room of his mother's house thinks of those who have been within its walls and others with whom he has had contact outside: "Alone, he was yet not alone, uniting as he did the themes of so many other lives" (pp. 20, 333). But this recapitulation is not quite the end. Whereas he had reflected before the first occurrence of the passage that "there was never any means of communication with the faces in the street", after the second he goes out and finds the faces in the night buses "potentially communicative": having boarded a bus "He felt like someone who had been asleep, and had only just woken".

Elyot, it is implied, genuinely chooses life—a form of intensification through imaginatively entering into the lives of other people. Here, surely, is a hint of the theme taken up and given very surprising development in Part Two of *The Aunt's Story*. The trouble is that Elyot's choice is stated rather than demonstrated: we don't see him *experiencing* this intenser form of living, and nothing in the novel leads us to believe him capable of it. Moreover, hatred in this case almost overwhelms compassion: White responds imaginatively far more to the boredom and horror of the dead than to the glory of the living, and the simple carpenter Joe Barnett, a character built according to Lawrentian formula rather than comprehended from within, is inadequate to suggest the "ecstasy" that should balance the "sickness".

There is nothing factitious about *The Aunt's Story*, however, no suggestion of contrivance in reaching a neat resolu-

[6] "The Four Novels of Patrick White", *Meanjin*, XV (1956), p. 160.

tion. A new discipline in style matches the inner certainty of the writer as he examines the relation between wisdom and suffering, and the full weight of his theme is carried by Theodora Goodman, who is one of White's most finely and fully realized characters.

In Part One, "Meroë", we see the child whose vision would not exclude the grub in the heart of the rose become the middle-aged spinster too honest to marry Huntly Clarkson, the loved aunt and unloved daughter who "came when the voice called" (p. 9). Since she is denied the joys of a creative artist her intelligence and sensibility are a source of anguish to her except in "moments of insight" shared chiefly with her father, but also with people like the Man who was Given his Dinner and the Greek 'cellist Moraïtis, with whom she experiences affinity in a brief moment of contact. The happiness she enjoys in her father's company and her love for her home are beautifully implied by the account of their riding together:

> She listened to the clinking of the stirrups, and the horses blowing out their nostrils, and the heavy, slow, lazy streams of sound that fell from the coarse hair of their swishing tails. Theodora looked at the land that was theirs. There was peace of mind enough on Meroë. You could feel it, whatever it was, and you were not certain, but in your bones. It was in the clothes-line on which the sheets drooped, in the big pink and yellow cows cooling their heels in creek mud, in magpie's speckled egg, and the disappearing snake. It was even in the fences, grey with age and yellow with lichen, that tumbled down and lay round Meroë. The fences were the last word in peace of mind. (pp. 23-24)

—a passage which illuminates her later statement of faith to Sokolnikov: "I believe in a pail of milk . . ." (p. 159).

Her father's death, described with a moving brevity and restraint, is the beginning of Theodora's alienation from the world: other relationships, with Frank Parrott and Huntly Clarkson, the men she might have married, she terminates herself by the shooting of the hawk and the clay ducks, acts which emphasize her separateness. After the shooting of the hawk, with which she had identified herself, "I was wrong, she said, but I shall continue to destroy myself, right down to the last of my several lives" (pp. 73-74). Even with her niece

Lou, Theodora is conscious of "the distance that separates" (p. 137), though with Lou, who is so like her in various ways but has "no obvious connexion" with either of her parents, she has a special relationship which is adroitly suggested by juxtaposition rather than stated. The paragraph in which Fanny's pregnancy is announced immediately follows one describing Theodora's sensations after Moraïtis's concert:

... the music which Moraïtis had played was more tactile than the hot words of lovers spoken on a wild nasturtium bed, the violins had arms. This thing which had happened between Moraïtis and herself she held close, like a woman holding her belly. She smiled. If I were an artist, she said, I would create something that would answer him. Or if I were meant to be a mother, it would soon smile in my face. But although she was neither of these, her contentment filled the morning ... (p. 117)

Here in germ is the idea of the relation of the spiritual lovers Voss and Laura to Rose Portion's child, but much more discreetly handled than the elaboration of the idea in physical terms in *Voss*.

The other characters in this first part of the novel are outlined with clarity and precision, and White's wit in presenting the alien, commonplace world outside Theodora's secret life has a poise and certainty of touch lacking in some of his later satirical passages: of Fanny, for instance: "You remembered the flesh of early roses, but under the skin you could read arithmetic" (p. 86). And how well he places the destructive Mrs Goodman in the early pages—the woman born as Theodora suggests with an axe in her hand, whose great tragedy was "that she had never done a murder. Her husband had escaped into the ground, and Theodora into silences" (p. 99), who could however kill happiness in a breath:

Once there were the new dresses that were put on for Mother's sake.
"Oh," she cried, "Fanny, my roses, my roses, you are very pretty."
Because Fanny was as pink and white as roses in the new dress.
"And Theo," she said, "all dressed up. Well, well. But I don't think we'll let you wear yellow again, because it doesn't suit, even in a sash. It turns you sallow," Mother said. (pp. 26-27)

In White's later novels and short stories there is increasing evidence of an unresolved conflict between the points of view of the visionary and the connoisseur: if all that matters is qualifying for a seat in the chariot, why care, it may be asked, whether people know the difference between an Aubusson carpet and Wilton wall-to-wall, or prefer texture-brick to stone? Yet in *Riders in the Chariot* it almost seems as though Mrs Jolley is evil *because* she likes pastel shades. Mrs Goodman's evil qualities are much more solidly based.

Unlike her sister Fanny, of whom their father says that "Fanny would always ask the questions that have answers" (p. 40), Theodora reaches out for deeper experience. At the end of this section she makes a great advance in self-knowledge in recognizing the "core of evil" in her from which springs her hostility to her mother and the necessity of destroying "the great monster Self", but she also realizes that she has not yet the humility needed. The rest of the book shows the process by which she attains that humility.

When Theodora goes to Europe after her mother's death and enriches her mental experience by entering in imagination into the lives of the amusing and pathetic eccentrics at her Riviera hotel, where in the symbolic jardin exotique "the soul, left with little to hide behind, must . . . come out into the open" (p. 146), she experiences "the great fragmentation of maturity"[7] of which the epigraph from Henry Miller speaks, discovering, as Holstius points out later, that these "created lives" are interchangeable, "the faces . . . only slightly different aspects of the same state" (p. 188). They take on aspects of people she has known—Katina of Lou, for instance —but also of Theodora herself: if Katina shares her more attractive qualities, Lieselotte possesses her destructive impulses. In this bubble world of unreason, both sinister and comic, the inconsequential dialogue has a kind of wild sense: as when Mrs Rapallo bids the General after the breaking of the nautilus: "Go, hang out your soul to dry. You Russians were always damp" (p. 225). Her confession that her daughter the Principessa does not exist, and General Sokolnikov's that he is only a major, undermine this life of illusion by letting in a measure of reality: and it is finally terminated by

---

[7] Cf. the comment on the Parkers in *The Tree of Man*: "It was obvious that these lives had never shattered into coloured fragments" (p. 95).

the destructive and purgatorial fire, in which the acquisitive Demoiselles Bloch lose their possessions and those subject to consuming passions their lives.

The epigraph to Part Three ("When your life is most real, to me you are mad") points to the hazard of talking, as most critics do, of Theodora's madness in the latter part of the novel. White avoids such simple labels.[8] "Who's crazy and who isn't? Can you tell me that?" the Man who was Given his Dinner had asked (p. 45). (The doctor who takes charge of Theodora pointedly refers to her condition as *lucidity*.) As Marjorie Barnard has said: "The world is arraigned, not Theodora."[9]

Walking with Sokolnikov between the sea and the houses, Theodora had perceived in the landscape that there was "no break in the continuity of being" (p. 188). By the beginning of Part Three, when as she writes to Fanny "I have seen and done", her awareness of the difference between doing and being enables her to recognize, as she journeys across America, an "integrity of purpose and of being" in "the full golden theme of corn" and the "counter-point of houses", whereas she herself is a discord: there is "no safeguard against the violence of personality" (p. 274). Her decision is announced abruptly: "Then, in a gust, Theodora knew that her abstraction also did not fit"—so she gets off the train and finally takes refuge in the empty house. Must she mortify herself to the very end? the reader who is neither saint nor mystic may be tempted to ask. But from the first compromise has been shown to be unnatural to Theodora: the sudden decision, implicit in what we already know of her, commands assent.

To strip oneself of inessentials is a necessary preliminary for illumination. Theodora when she reached the Hôtel du Midi took out objects of her own (few and simple though they were) "to give the room her identity" (p. 144), but now when she abandons the train she throws away her tickets and even gives herself a false name: "This way perhaps she came a little closer to humility, to anonymity, to pureness of being"

---

[8] Cf. Blake: "as I was walking among the fires of hell, delighted with the enjoyments of Genius, which to Angels look like torment and insanity . . ." (*The Marriage of Heaven and Hell*).

[9] "Theodora Again", *Southerly*, XX (1959), p. 54.

(p. 284). And so she is prepared for the "ultimate moment of clear vision", when Holstius, that imaginary composite of the men from whom she has learned wisdom, tells her she must accept the two irreconcilable halves, joy and sorrow, flesh and marble, illusion and reality, life and death: "And you have already found that . . . there is sometimes little to choose between the reality of illusion and the illusion of reality" (p. 293). Though she has to defer to those who prescribe the reasonable life and insist on taking her into custody, Theodora wins the game for her soul.

This search for "pureness of being"—which is ultimately to prove, in the words of *Little Gidding*, "A condition of complete simplicity (Costing not less than everything)"—is a recurring theme in White's work, from the early short story "The Twitching Colonel" to *Riders in the Chariot*. Colonel Trevellick, a retired Indian Army officer, affirms that "Only in dissolution is salvation from illusion": "I shall strip myself, the onion-folds of prejudice, till standing naked though conscious I see myself complete or else consumed like the Hindu conjuror who is translated into space", whereas Maud, his wife, had been, he reflects, "attached to her self beyond escaping".[10] And a similar image is used by Miss Hare: "Eventually I shall discover what is at the centre, if enough of me is peeled away".[11]

Theodora, then, like Voss, goes forth on a journey which is also a journey of spiritual discovery: but whereas Voss is the explorer, Theodora is the traveller wandering in the Old and New Worlds. And this points to the significance of White's use of the *Odyssey* motif.

The landscape of Part One of *The Aunt's Story* is said to have been suggested by the country round Moss Vale,[12] though, characteristically, White does not obtrude local references: it is also a symbolic landscape associating Meroë, the Goodman home, with both Ethiopia and the Greek islands, by means of the skeleton trees, described as "the abstractions

---

[10] "The Twitching Colonel", *The London Mercury* (April 1937), pp. 606, 607.

[11] *Riders in the Chariot* (1961), p. 57.

[12] Peter Hastings, "The Writing Business" (Sydney *Observer*, 21st March 1959).

of trees, with their roots in Ethiopia", and the live trees, "a solid majority of soughing pines" (p. 20), later associated with the stunted pines of Greece. (It is relevant to recall that *The Aunt's Story* was written shortly after Patrick White had spent a year in Greece: during the war he had been stationed for a time in Northern Africa.) In a passage referring to the foreign books which Theodora's father used to read (p. 22), two authors are named: Herodotus and Homer, and there is mention of the story of the crocodile and the trochilus which Herodotus tells in his second volume, dealing with Egypt. In an earlier chapter of that volume, just after discussing the mystery of the sources of the Nile, Herodotus speaks of the Ethiopian capital, a great city called Meroë, on an island of the same name, though he does not describe it in detail. At first Theodora rejects the thought of the second Meroë, but in time it becomes "a dim and accepted apprehension lying quietly at the back of the mind" (p. 23). Later through Moraïtis she perceives an analogy between Meroë and Greece, each being a country of bones. This association is stressed by the image of the pines, the emotional value of which is made explicit in the reference in *Riders in the Chariot* to "a scent of pine needles, the waves of which, at the best of times, will float their victims back into the intolerable caverns of nostalgia" (p. 201). In *The Aunt's Story*, they suggest Ithaca, the goal of Odysseus' journey: it is also relevant, since Ithaca is as it were an aspect of Meroë, that Milton's Mount Amara,[13] "by som suppos'd True Paradise",[14] is situated in Abyssinia ("where *Abassin* Kings thir issue Guard . . . under the *Ethiop* Line By *Nilus* head")?

From the days of the early commentators on Homer the *Odyssey* has been frequently interpreted allegorically, for example, by the Neoplatonists, and George Chapman, working out his own interpretation of Ulysses reaching spiritual greatness through the endurance of adversity, wrote in his commentary on his translation: "The information or fashion of an absolute man, and necessarie (or fatal) passage through many afflictions (according with the most sacred Letter) to his

---

[13] This is discussed by J. L. Lowes in *The Road to Xanadu*, immediately after his reference on pp. 373-4 to Bruce's account of the island of Meroë.
[14] *Paradise Lost*, IV. 280-3.

naturall haven and countrey, is the whole argument and scope of this inimitable and miraculous Poeme."

The example of Joyce in describing a spiritual quest within a Homeric framework inevitably springs to mind, since he is certainly one of the major shaping influences on White's early work, as seen for instance in the experiments in stream of consciousness from "The Twitching Colonel" onwards and perhaps in the theme of *The Living and the Dead* (it is surely not mere coincidence that the words of that title are also the concluding words of Joyce's story *The Dead?*). The use of recurrent imagery and symbolic colours[15] in *The Aunt's Story* itself probably owes something to his example. Even if it were *Ulysses*, however, and not simply the Greek landscape which prompted White's use of the *Odyssey* motif, his method is individual. He does not attempt anything like the elaborate structural parallels of *Ulysses*, but by allusion and image uses the *Odyssey* as a means of indirectly defining character and theme and as a kind of short-cut to emotional intensity. It may not be fanciful to detect occasional echoes in the story itself: in Part Three Theodora stripping herself of all her possessions recalls Odysseus returning to Ithaca in the disguise of a beggarman, the greeting given her by the Johnsons' scruffy red dog suggests Odysseus' welcome from his old dog Argus; when Mrs Johnson brings Theodora water to wash herself, just before she gives herself a false name, we may remember Odysseus' old nurse washing his feet and recognizing him. But what White is concerned with is pointing up his theme by a very free method of allusion: the significance often lies in the variations and reversals.

The motif is introduced in relation to Theodora's father, who reads in a room on the side of the house where the pines are: ". . . the perpetual odyssey on which George Goodman was embarked, on which the purple water swelled beneath the keel, rising and falling like the wind in pines on the blue shore of Ithaca" (p. 68). A romantic dreamer, he talks to Theodora of Nausicaä, a name "as smooth and straight and tough as an arrow", then suddenly realizes that he has a daughter of his own: "she has grown, he said, straight as a

---

[15] The colour symbolism was first pointed out by Marjorie Barnard in her review in *Southerly*, XX (1959), 51-55.

brown arrow" (p. 69). The allusions, while, in the second case, conferring a grace on Theodora, reveal George Goodman as very unlike Odysseus, the clear-eyed man of action. His tragedy is that although he travels he never sees Greece, he cannot escape from his Penelope, whereas Mrs Goodman's world "had always been enclosed, her Ithaca, and here she would have kept the suitors at bay, not through love and patience, but with suitable conversation and a stick" (p. 93).

Theodora herself, as well as being at one point Nausicaä, at others is connected both with Telemachus and with Odysseus. In the early scenes with her father, sharing his life on their estate, she plays Telemachus to his Odysseus, and mourns the dwindling of Meroë as Telemachus mourns the wasting of his substance by the suitors—but here, ironically, it is Odysseus himself who is responsible for the decay: and at the end of the story, when she finds a father-figure in Holstius, the reminders of George Goodman[16] add greatly to the poignancy of these final scenes. When Theodora has to leave Meroë after her father's death it becomes identified in her mind with Ithaca. At her meeting with their former servant, Pearl Brawne, who reminds her of her father and the past, the imagery, drawn from Odysseus' encounter with the Sirens, suggests the irresistible power of her memories: "Theodora would have blocked her ears with wax. She could not bear to face the islands from which Pearl sang" (p. 133).

Having embarked on her odyssey, Theodora hopes when she reaches the Hôtel du Midi that the garden will be "the goal of a journey", for hitherto she has been disappointed in her travels through "the gothic shell of Europe . . . in which the ghosts of Homer and St Paul and Tolstoy waited for the crash" (pp. 145, 146); but the hotel itself is part of the "gothic shell". The atmosphere of decadence recalls the world of *The Living and the Dead*: it is not until she reaches the New World that Theodora attains her final vision. Homer, St Paul and Tolstoy are, I suppose, associated as each representing a type of spiritual quest: they contribute to the pattern of this section, Homer through the *Odyssey* theme, St Paul through Theodora's reading of the *Acts*, Tolstoy because parts of it are like a parody of the Platonic Idea of a Russian novel (and

[16] For instance, on his second appearance Holstius wears a Panama hat.

this perhaps is the point of the rather surprising information that Mrs Goodman could read Russian).

At the end of Part Two the Nostos theme is sounded. Theodora, purged by fire, decides to go home, but it is not now the blue shore of Ithaca but the black volcanic hills of Ethiopia which summon her: Fanny is startled to receive a letter saying "the time has come at last to return to Abyssinia" (p. 271). The final and most radical manipulation of the *Odyssey* theme is still to come, however: having travelled far and learnt much, this wanderer does not return home after all. The end of Theodora's quest is to make her independent of places as of people. Soon after her father's death she wrote to her friend Violet Adams: "At first I thought I could not live anywhere but at Meroë, and that Meroë was my bones and breath, but now I begin to suspect that any place is habitable, depending, of course, on the unimportance of one's life" (p. 90). Finally, as people become interchangeable in her mind, so places. When she goes off on her own up the mountain road she finds herself "walking between pines, or firs, anyway some kind of small coniferous tree, stunted and dark" (p. 277); and the lonely house in which she takes refuge is described in terms ("a thin house, with elongated windows, like a lantern" [p. 289]) recalling the madman's folly near Meroë, "a narrow lantern" near the summit of a hill, "the black cone of Ethiopia that had once flowed fire" (p. 61).

It will be clear from my discussion of the *Odyssey* theme that the use of recurring images is an important feature of *The Aunt's Story*—one which James McAuley[17] and Marjorie Barnard[18] have briefly noted. Throughout White constructs an extraordinary reticulation of images—roses, bones, the clock, tables and chairs, fire, zinc—which by repetition, juxtaposition and contrast acquire symbolic value.[19] Thus the wooden images, commented on by McAuley, which are used

[17] See his review in *Quadrant*, 12 (1959), p. 91.
[18] "The Four Novels of Patrick White", *Meanjin*, XV (1956), 165. See also H. P. Heseltine, "Patrick White's Style", *Quadrant*, 27 (1963), 61-74.
[19] White is reported to have said: "Music helps me with the structure of a book". (Ian Moffitt, "Talk with Patrick White", *New York Times Book Review*, 18th August 1957). This use of images like musical themes is obviously an example.

to suggest the physical appearance of Theodora, her angular honesty, and the wooden box of her personality which encloses her except in rare moments of spiritual exaltation, are frequently contrasted with images of flowing and of fire. The knife, which first appears unobtrusively as the little silver paper knife which Mrs Goodman mislays at the time when Theodora has Frank Parrott at her mercy and which is found again after his engagement to Fanny, figures again as the meat-knife with which Jack Frost cut the throats of his wife and children—an incident, apparently irrelevant, introduced proleptically for its thematic value before the culminating appearance of the knife which Theodora picks up when tempted to kill her mother.

White clearly wants his symbols to work by poetic suggestion rather than the rigid consistency of allegory: the risks involved are ambiguity and obscurity. In the Odyssean context Theodora's large and timeless hats might suggest a traveller, but they may simply signify identity, as when she deliberately leaves behind the hat with the black gauze rose which Mrs Johnson uncomprehendingly returns to her. Again, there is a danger of ambiguity when the symbols acquire different moral connotations in different contexts. When Lou, "as unpredictable as water", is contrasted with her brothers, whom "you could have piled into two heaps of stones" (p. 15), it is clear that Lou's spiritual potentialities are much greater, and there is no question that fluidity is preferable to rigidity. But when Theodora, wearing "a long, an oblong dress", goes to the Agricultural Show with two fashionable women, and her attitudes are "those of carved wood" whereas "the powdered, silky, instinctively insinuating bodies of the other women flowed" (p. 122), the moral values implicit in the contrast are reversed.

Even if abundance occasionally becomes excess, the images are of great value in linking the parts of the novel and tracing a significant pattern. The symbol of the rose, for instance, expands through its use in different contexts, gathering accretions of meaning. It is first used in the description of Meroë, in association with the skeleton trees and the pines: the *artificial* rose garden situated (oddly for Australia?) on the south side of the house and made at the behest of Mrs Goodman in clay carted specially from a great distance. Theodora sees the reflection of the roses in bed and for her they become a symbol of beauty. She remembers her happy childhood at Meroë as "an epoch of roselight" (p. 21), and later contrasts herself unfavourably with Fanny and Pearl Brawne, both of whom resemble roses: but the exquisite Fanny's appearance is deceptive and Pearl is soon overblown. At the Hôtel du Midi the maroon paper roses in her bedroom are associated with lust and meretriciousness: finally Theodora wears the hat with the black gauze rose, also artificial, "more a sop to convention than an attempt at beauty" (p. 274), but black like Theodora herself.[20]

The way in which White by juxtaposing images can enrich their meaning and draw his themes together is well illustrated in the description of Huntly Clarkson's dinner party for Moraïtis:

Huntly's table was smouldering with red roses, the roselight that Theodora remembered now, of Meroë. She swam through the sea of roses towards that other Ithaca. On that side there were the pines, and on this side Moraïtis. (p. 111)

The imagery alone tells much about the state of Theodora's feelings and the significance for her of this encounter with Moraïtis.

An interesting example of the metamorphosis of an image in different contexts occurs first in the description of Theodora carrying her baby niece: "beautiful as stone, in her stone arms the gothic child", and, a moment later after Fanny claims the child, "ugly as stone, awkwardness in her empty hands" (p. 119). A few pages later this scene is recalled when Theodora tells her mother that she won a kewpie in a feather skirt at the Show, and Mrs Goodman imagines her carrying it through the crowd: "In her hate she would have hewn down this great wooden idol with the grotesque doll in its arms" (p. 126). Occurring so soon after the image of Theodora as a Madonna with Child, it carries the suggestion that in winning the kewpie she has in effect ended her own chance of maternity, since the episode virtually ends her relationship with Huntly Clarkson.

[20] Cf. the roses "as brown as paper bags" of the Ethiopian Meroë (p. 23).

Adverse criticism of *The Aunt's Story* has tended to concentrate on Part Two: Vincent Buckley for instance has applied the phrase "a soft cocoon of imprecision"[21] to the prose here. That there should be a change to a more fluid style as we pass from reality to illusion is however appropriate: and as Theodora lives her fantasy life her vision naturally assumes a dreamlike quality. For instance, Pearl Brawne in Part One is described in images which suggest what she looked like to Theodora, but one feels that she sees what any sensitive observer might see:

... you looked up through Pearl, and it was like looking through a golden forest in which the sun shone. Pearl was beautiful. Pearl was big and gold. Her hair was thick heavy stuff, as coarse as a mare's plaited tail. It hung and swung, golden and heavy, when she let it down. (p. 34)

whereas we see Sokolnikov through the eyes of a woman whose vision is peculiar to herself:

The General sighed as deeply and as endlessly as cotton wool, but when he smacked his lips, or sucked from his fingers whatever it was, the suction of rubber sprang into the room, out of his face, for this was rubber in the manner of the faces of most Russians. His lips would fan out into a rubber trumpet down which poured the rounded stream of words . . .(p. 156)

Part Two is certainly difficult, a bold experiment in rendering the mental life of Theodora by a more dramatic method of blending past and present, illusion and reality than ordinary interior monologue. On a chance remark Theodora will build a fantasy of the past involving herself, as when Katina's reference to an earthquake prompts her to imagine herself as the governess of the child Katina, experiencing that earthquake; or memories of her own past will attach themselves to present happenings, as when Katina proposes a picnic: " 'I dare say it will be made,' Theodora Goodman said wryly, remembering another stiff group beside the church" (p. 232)—that is, her disappointment as a schoolgirl when Frank Parrott after church one day proposed a picnic

---

[21] "Patrick White and His Epic", *Twentieth Century*, XII (1958), p. 246, an article reprinted in *Australian Literary Criticism*, ed. Grahame Johnston, O.U.P. (1962).

which he promptly forgot. When the General speaks of his mannish sister Ludmilla, Theodora smiles "because her boots rang hollow on the cold yellow grass, and in her armpit she felt the firmness of her little rifle" (p. 156), which implies without any authorial intrusion that Theodora not only identifies herself with Ludmilla but also associates the General with her father. A still stranger transformation occurs when after she reads her Testament she and the General figure as Lukich and his younger brother Pavel in an adventure with some Russians, one of whom is called Petya, to whom the General, discoursing on the Russian Revolution, proclaims that "A movement requires a rock" (p. 216). When she speculates whether the walls of the round tower enclose "the smell of nettles, and possibly a dead bird, some personal exaltation or despair" (p. 251), the images recall the emotions associated with the discovery of Pearl and Tom among the nettles and of the dead crow beneath the pew, and with the shooting of the little hawk.

The Aunt's Story is the work in which White has advanced furthest towards the frontiers of poetry. It is perhaps true that a novel cannot well bear the strain of such a complex pattern of symbolic imagery: in the larger novels that have followed there has necessarily been a loosening of texture in the prose, which in *Riders in the Chariot* has become a more flexible narrative medium, though there has also been an increase in syntactical eccentricities from which *The Aunt's Story* is relatively free. It is also true, however, that the kind of vision which White is trying to embody in this book demands the subtlest and richest use of language for its realization. *The Aunt's Story* asks careful reading: that it deserves it is the proof of its quality.

1/1965

Patrick White's
The Tree of Man

G. A. WILKES

After the accomplishment of *The Aunt's Story*, *The Tree of Man* (1955) seems an awkward, experimental book. The two novels are separated by an interval of seven years, the years of silence that followed White's return to Australia in 1948. As he explained in his personal note, "The Prodigal Son",[1] demobilization in England had left him with the alternatives of remaining in "what I then felt to be an actual and spiritual graveyard, with the prospect of ceasing to be an artist and turning instead into that most sterile of beings, a London intellectual", or of returning home, "to the stimulus of time remembered". He chose to return. Taking up a farm at Castle Hill, White allowed the idea of writing to remain dormant, while he absorbed himself in growing flowers and vegetables, and in breeding Schnauzers and Saanen goats. "The first years I was content with these activities, and to soak myself in landscape . . . Nothing seemed important, beyond living and eating, with a roof of one's own over one's head."

The silence was broken eventually by the need to answer a question White asked himself. "Returning sentimentally to a country I had left in my youth, what had I really found?"

In all directions stretched the Great Australian Emptiness, in which the mind is the least of possessions, in which the rich man is the important man, in which the schoolmaster and the journalist rule what intellectual roost there is, in which beautiful youths and

---

[1] *Australian Letters*, I, iii (1958), 37-40. All quotations in the first three paragraphs are from this source. Quotations from *The Tree of Man* are from the English edition (Eyre and Spottiswoode, 1956).

girls stare at life through blind blue eyes, in which human teeth fall like autumn leaves, the buttocks of cars grow hourly glassier, food means cake and steak, muscles prevail, and the march of material ugliness does not raise a quiver from the average nerves.

It was the exaltation of the "average" that made me panic most, and in this frame of mind, in spite of myself, I began to conceive another novel. Because the void I had to fill was so immense, I wanted to try to suggest in this book every possible aspect of life, through the lives of an ordinary man and woman. But at the same time I wanted to discover the extraordinary behind the ordinary, the mystery and the poetry which alone could make bearable the lives of such people, and incidentally, my own life since my return.

So I began to write *The Tree of Man*.

The attempt to confront The Great Australian Emptiness persists in *Voss*, and assumes another aspect ("the buttocks of cars grow hourly glassier") in the satire on suburbia in *Riders in the Chariot* and *The Season at Sarsaparilla*. In *The Tree of Man* itself, however, the effort is still to see "even the ugliness, the bags and iron of Australian life", with a redeeming vision. The reversion to the pioneering novel is itself a turning away from life in its more civilized and artificial forms, as though essential values are being sought elsewhere. White acknowledged that his own conception of writing had changed completely, so that what had once meant "the practice of an art by a polished mind in civilized surroundings", became now "a struggle to create completely fresh forms out of the rocks and sticks of words".

The sense of struggle and pressure in the prose of *The Tree of Man*—a contrast to the "Meroë" section of *The Aunt's Story*—is yet made to serve the vision the book imposes. The narrative begins with an unnamed man driving in his cart into the solitude of the bush, building a fire to thrust back the cold and the dark, and sharing his meal with his dog. The prose is commanding in its rhythm and selection of detail, compelling assent to the illusion it creates:

> Night had settled on the small cocoon of light, threatening to crush it. The cold air flowing sluiced the branches of trees, surged through the standing trunks, and lay coldly mounting in the gully. Rocks groaned with cold. In the saucers that pocked the face of stone, water tightened and cracked.

A frosty, bloody hole, complained the man, from out of the half-sleep in which he had become involved, and twitched the bags tighter round his body.

But he knew also there was nothing to be done. He knew that where his cart had stopped, he would stop. There was nothing to be done. He would make the best of this cell in which he had been locked. How much of will, how much of fate, entered into this it was difficult to say. Or perhaps fate is will. Anyway, Stan Parker was pretty stubborn. (p. 7)

Stan Parker builds a shack in the clearing, and brings a woman to share his life with him; the stages in their relationship will be marked by a storm, a flood, and a bushfire; and meanwhile as the circles widen, the shack becomes part of a settlement, then of the wider community, Durilgai, with its post-office and general store. The opening chapters of *The Tree of Man* are masterful in presenting the man and the woman as inseparable from the activities in which they are engaged, so that anyone impinging on their closed existence —like the stranger with the magnetical water, or the boy from the flood—seems almost a symbolic event. White shows the simplicity of the life of Stan and Amy Parker, at the same time making it seem timeless and universal.

As the narrative advances, however, the Parkers are seen more in their relationships to others—to the O'Dowds and Quigleys, to their children Ray and Thelma—and also especially in their relationship to each other. They are both inarticulate figures to whom thought is painful, and who are most often baffled by what their experience might imply. The novel relies for much of its strength on White's feeling for the awkwardness and fumblings of human relationships, Amy unable to express her love for Stan as he leaves for market except by calling "And there's a slice of pie beneath the sandwiches" (p. 28), or her feeling on his return except by pointing out that his coat has become hitched up at the back. The dialogue between the two is most expressive when it communicates something quite other than what they are saying, with Stan perhaps treadling the grindstone and replying without speaking or lifting his head. The Parkers are pathetic and yet noble as their children draw away from them, Thelma to cultivate a shallow gentility and Ray to escape his sense of persecution in a life of crime: the contrast between the generations gives the limited and imperceptive lives of Stan and Amy a moving integrity.

In measuring in this way the disillusion of middle age, in showing so poignantly the failure of contact between people who spend their lives together, *The Tree of Man* has an essential quality of insight and compassion beside which its "saga" framework seems distracting and inflated. It is true that the storm, flood, bushfire and drought are not introduced simply as the clichés of the pioneering novel, but to mark phases in the history of the Parkers and endow it with an epic quality. In the same way the title of the book recalls Housman's "On Wenlock Edge the wood's in trouble", where a man watching a gale blow through the trees reflects that centuries before, in Roman Britain, another man may have seen the same sight and thought the same thoughts:

> There, like the wind through woods in riot,
>   Through him the gale of life blew high;
> The tree of man was never quiet:
>   Then 'twas the Roman, now 'tis I.
>   (*A Shropshire Lad*, XXXI)

As the wood has preserved an identity down the centuries, despite the wind blowing through it, the life of man has a continuity also—so that all that the Parkers failed to achieve, and the hopes that their children betrayed, may be fulfilled in their grandson.

"I wanted to try to suggest in this book every possible aspect of life, through the lives of an ordinary man and woman." *The Tree of Man* must be praised for the gallantry of the attempt rather than for the sureness of its achievement. We have a greater awareness of the essential nature of Stan's experience when he is not contending with a bushfire or a flood, but making his awkward journey to the city to assume responsibility for what Ray has done; Amy's disenchantment in middle life is conveyed more forcibly in her resentment of Stan, as someone imagined holding a secret denied to her, than through the season of drought in the natural order. There is a disturbing feeling that the Parkers are being *sent* a drought, a storm, a fire and a world war in the hope of evoking some response from them, while they themselves seem to be going through these events like sleepwalkers, instead of experiencing them fully. The strength of the book lies in its human relationships, which are weakened by the attempt to extend them into a "myth". For this reason the theme of continuity hinted in the title also remains nominal, and its intrusion at the close does not accord with the stronger impression made by the action itself.

The coherence of *The Tree of Man* comes from the predicament of the Parkers, two commonplace lives analysed at greater length and in more detail than any other novelist has attempted. They are both presented as obscure to themselves, awaiting some revelation or fulfilment that does not seem to come. The mythic framework is sometimes relevant to this theme of fulfilment, but more often a distraction. It is half-implied that Stan has been named after Stanley the explorer, and he journeys into the bush with his horse and his dog in resistance to his mother's upbringing, because "the souls of human beings . . . will burst out of any box they are put inside" (p. 6). He glimpses a larger life through reading *Hamlet*, or through the stories of the Gold Coast told by the stranger with the magnetical water:

> Stan Parker was torn between the images of gold and ebony and his own calm life of flesh. He did not wish to take his hat from the peg and say, Well, so long, I'm off to see foreign places. This did not bring the sweat to the backs of his knees. He had a subtler longing. It was as if the beauty of the world had risen in a sleep, in the crowded wooden room, and he could almost take it in his hands. All words that he had never expressed might suddenly be spoken. He had in him great words of love and beauty, below the surface, if they could be found.
>
> But all he said was, again, "The Gold Coast, eh?" And reached for the bottle. (p. 35)

Amy Parker feels excluded from the conversation of the men. Her Gold Coast is found in objects like the silver nutmeg-grater given her as a wedding present, which seems the loveliest thing she has ever seen. In the morning she discovers that the stranger has apparently stolen it.

The stranger peddling Bibles and magnetical water is the first of the minor lives that intersect the Parkers'. The next is the woman in the cart who pulls up to notice Amy's rosebush. "Gingerbread never got anyone nowheres," Mrs O'Dowd announces, holding instead to "the pigs, two sow in farrer, and a pretty young boar, and the pullets besides" (p. 40). The arrival of the O'Dowds is followed shortly by the appearance of the Quigleys, with whom the experience of the Parkers is to be more subtly interwoven. Doll Quigley is the tall and angular woman who is given respect even though she goes barefoot, and looks after her idiot brother all her life, then kills him when she can do so no longer. Bub Quigley, with his rapt smile, gazes into the faces of the corpses salvaged from the Wullunya flood, and looks into the faces of the living "with such candour that it became obvious that he was mingling with their thoughts" (p. 84). A little later Amy encounters Mr Gage, the eccentric husband of the postmistress, kneeling in the road staring at an ant. When Mr Gage eventually hangs himself with two belts in his backyard, his wife reveals his horrible paintings—including a Christ-figure looking like a plucked fowl—to show the other women what she has had to endure. (Mrs Gage appears again at the end, set up in a modern home through selling the work of her husband's genius, and just finished paying off the fridge.)

It does violence to White's art to single out these episodes from their context, but the lives of the Quigleys, the O'Dowds and the Gages are variations on his main theme, suggesting possibilities latent in the experience of Stan and Amy or helping to define its singularity. Amy Parker is the more bewildered and resentful: her plight is imaged in Mr Gage's painting of a laborious naked woman reaching up with ponderous hands to a savagely dazzling sun. "The mystery and the poetry" (in White's words) that make bearable the lives of ordinary people Amy wants to hold and possess in small articles like a silver nutmeg-grater, or to domesticate in the form of a rosebush. She tries to capture the romantic and exotic by living the lives of others by proxy, as she does in projecting herself into the life of Madeleine, the cream-complexioned woman on the glittering house. In the same way she imagines herself making love to Tom Armstrong, and then is unfaithful in fact with Leo the commercial traveller. Amy's craving *is* to possess, and she becomes resentful because Stan somehow eludes her, has an existence independently that she cannot annihilate in her own. It is also partly the resentment that the ordinary person feels towards the visionary, and it will recur in Reha Himmelfarb's attitude to her husband (as though he had a secret knowledge he would not share with her), and in Mrs Jolley's developing hatred of Miss Hare.

Stan Parker is the mute visionary in *The Tree of Man*. He represents an element in the book that critics have shied away from, even though it is a central element, and one persistent in White's work from the beginning. Stan's soul has refused to stay in the box in which his mother tried to put it; intimations of worlds beyond his experience come to him from reading Shakespeare, or hearing talk of "gold and ebony" on a stranger's lips; as he goes about his work on the evening after the thunderstorm, he is half-aware of a revelation that has approached, but has not yet come:

> He was tired. He was also at peace under the orange sky. Events had exhausted him. He had not learned to think far, and in what progress he had made had reached the conclusion he was a prisoner in his human mind, as in the mystery of the natural world. Only sometimes the touch of hands, the lifting of a silence, the sudden shape of a tree or presence of a first star, hinted at eventual release.
> But not now. And he did not ask for it. (p. 46)

The "eventual release" from the prison of Stan's human mind is akin to the illumination that came to Theodora Goodman. As a girl at Meroë, Theodora felt her identity slipping away from her as she entered the being of the little hawk with the red eye, or as her personality dissolved in the movement of the dance. Theodora's progress through *The Aunt's Story* was towards "that desirable state . . . which resembles, one would imagine, nothing more than air or water" (p. 151), the state she achieved finally in the extinction of reason.

The Aunt's Story had questioned the value of life in the terms in which it is normally lived, and in the solitariness of Theodora at the end, implied a rejection of life in such terms. This tendency is resisted in *The Tree of Man*. It might almost have been written to put an end to the theme of "alienation" developing through White's earlier books. In 1947 he had conceived the play *The Ham Funeral*, which brought together two opposing principles in his work: in the Young Man, a full statement of the introverted, maladjusted personality, who is trying to find a refuge from the business of living; and in Mrs Lusty—anticipated in Catherine Standish, and to be extended in Nola Boyle and Daise Morrow—a character standing for that acceptance of life at any level from which the Young Man shrinks. The crisis of the play is the confrontation of the two, thrusting upon the Young Man the responsibility of embracing life at its most squalid and frowsy and vulgar. What the play finally demonstrates, however, is the inadequacy of both views. True serenity and insight belong only to the landlord, Will Lusty, who asserts that "This table is love . . . if you can get to know it." He is the successor to Theodora Goodman, isolated from the other characters and inscrutable to them.

In *The Tree of Man*, with its emphasis on the ordinariness of Stan and Amy, and the commonplaceness of their lives, the acceptance of the workaday world is again being insisted upon. It is felt almost as a mystique in the early chapters of the book, as the Parkers are absorbed in the ritualistic milking of cows, or sense the cabbages tensing in the early light of the morning. White's exceptional powers with language here become uncertain of their effect:

> She buried her forehead in the cow's soft side, and there was a continual stirring, and the gentle cow smell. The whole air those evenings was soft with the smell of cow's breath, as if the blue tongue had slapped it on. The old cow stood wisely waiting. Her ears were held twitched back, as if she were pleased. Her brown eyes looked inward, it appeared. There were little dots of passive moisture on her granite-coloured nose. (pp. 52-53)
>
> All along the morning stood the ears of young cabbages. Those that the rabbits did not nibble off. In the clear morning of those early years the cabbages stood out for the woman more distinctly than other things, when they were not melting, in a tenderness of light.
>
> The young cabbages, that were soon a prospect of veined leaves, melted in the mornings of thawing frost. Their blue and purple flesh ran together with the silver of water, the jewels of light, in the smell of warming earth. But always tensing. Already in the hard,

later light the young cabbages were resistant balls of muscle . . . (pp. 26-27)

There is a feeling of something obsessive here, almost as though the author were writing to convince himself. It is plainly intended that fulfilment for the Parkers will be found in their immersion in the simplicities of their peasant-like existence, not in the way of solitariness and alienation followed by Theodora.

The influence of D. H. Lawrence on *The Tree of Man*, although so frequently detected, need not specifically concern us. It is enough to draw attention to the perils of the literary traditions in which White has now become involved. Stan typically achieves his moments of lucidity in the presence of elemental forces in nature. The novelist of the most original talent must look nervously back over his shoulder in these circumstances, and White is beset by difficulties not of his making as he shows Stan exalted by the fire at Glastonbury, or drenched and cleansed by the storm. The storm passage in Part Two is of capital importance for the understanding of the book, as Stan is at first exultant in the rain, and then feels his selfhood being attenuated:

He folded his wet arms, and this attitude added to his complacency. He was firm and strong, husband, father, and owner of cattle. He sat there touching his own muscular arms, for he had taken off his shirt during the heat and was wearing his singlet. But as the storm increased, his flesh had doubts, and he began to experience humility. The lightning, which could have struck open basalt, had, it seemed, the power to open souls. It was obvious in the yellow flash that something like this had happened, the flesh had slipped from his bones, and a light was shining in his cavernous skull.

The rain buffeted and ran off the limbs of the man seated on the edge of the veranda. In his new humility weakness and acceptance had become virtues. He retreated now, into the shelter of the veranda, humbly holding with his hand the wooden post that he had put there himself years before, and at this hour of the night he was quite grateful for the presence of the simple wood. As the rain sluiced his lands, and the fork of the lightning entered the crests of his trees. The darkness was full of wonder. Standing there somewhat meekly, the man could have loved something, someone, if he could have penetrated beyond the wood, beyond the moving darkness. But he could not, and in his confusion he prayed to God, not in specific petition, wordlessly almost, for the sake of company. Till he began to know every corner of the darkness, as if it were daylight, and he were in love with the heaving world, down to the last blade of wet grass. (p. 152)

This is the same dissolution of personality that Theodora had experienced, but its expression now is love—love for the heaving world, down to the last blade of grass.

This is not a vision foisted into the narrative, for it has been prepared for from the beginning, recalling the earlier storm which had left Stan a prisoner in his human mind, yet promised "eventual release". Any awkwardness comes rather from the embarrassing tradition of nature mysticism that the passage cannot fail to call to mind, and from the inherent difficulty of rendering mystical experience in terms that make it seem other than vacuous. This difficulty is all the greater because Stan is powerless to interpret or explore his experience, as he himself does not understand it. For him to possess this state more continuously would be to draw nearer to the condition of Bub Quigley, with his wet mouth and rapt smile. Nor does the unfocused love for the world that Stan feels become established as a positive force in the book. When the attempt is made to establish it, in the episode of Ossie Peabody and the heifer the morning after the storm, the effect is dangerously close to sentimental.

The strength of *The Tree of Man* comes not from Stan's achievement of illumination, so much as from his blunderings towards it, his bewilderment and uncertainty, his painful effort to interpret such knowledge as he is given. In all this Stan is a man who is finally alone, as Theodora had been. He holds to Amy as a kind of certainty in his life, but cannot share his deepest experiences with her; in trying to make contact with Ray, he causes the boy apprehension and embarrassment; in his old age he has the respect of Thelma and a kind of wordless communion with his grandson—but our more lasting impression is that Stan's true life is in "that solitary land of the individual experience, in which no fellow football is ever heard".[2] This is not the lot he seeks—his effort

---

[2] From the epigraph to *The Aunt's Story*.

is to share his knowledge, to communicate with his fellows—but it is the lot to which he comes. For all its insistence on the values of the workaday world, its mystique of man immersed in nature, *The Tree of Man* shows that fulfilment for Stan lies not within life as normally lived, but beyond it.

This is the source of an uncertainty in the book—the tension between what the novel is apparently advocating, and what it enacts—while at the same time it deepens its significance. For it is Stan himself who is caught in the pull of the two forces, holding fast to the realities he can see and touch, like the grain of freshly-planed wood, and yet entering into the fullness of his experience only through a liberation from them. The reconciliation of the contraries comes finally in the scene just before Stan's death, when another minor life crosses his, and the young evangelist approaches the old man in his chair on the grass.

"I wanted, when I saw you, sir, to bring to you the story of the Gospels," said the young man, "and of Our Lord. I wanted to tell you of my own experience, and how it is possible for the most unlikely to be saved."

The old man was most unhappy.

"I was a fettler. I don't know whether you know anything of conditions in the fettlers' camps," said the young man, whose experience was filling his eyes, even to the exclusion of his present mission, the old man.

The young evangelist began to present himself in the most complete nakedness.

"Drinking and whoring most week-ends," he said. "We would go down into the nearest settlement and carry back the drink. It was wine mostly. We would knock the necks off, we were craving for it that bad. The women would come up along the line, knowing where the camp was. There were black women too."

The old man was intensely unhappy.

When the young one had finished his orgasm, he presented the open palms of his hands and told how he had knelt upon his knees, and grace descended on him.

"This can happen to you too," he said, kneeling on one knee, and sweating at every pore.

The old man cleared his throat. "I'm not sure whether I am intended to be saved," he said . . .

"But the glories of salvation," persisted the evangelist, whose hair went up in even waves, "these great glories are everybody's for the asking, just by a putting out of the hand."

The old man fidgeted. He was not saying anything. Great glories were glittering in the afternoon. He had already been a little dazzled . . .

"Don't you believe in God, perhaps?" asked the evangelist, who had begun to look around him and to feel the necessity for some further stimulus of confession. "I can show you books," he yawned.

Then the old man, who had been cornered long enough, saw, through perversity perhaps, but with his own eyes. He was illuminated.

He pointed with his stick at the gob of spittle.

"That is God," he said.

As it lay glittering intensely and personally on the ground.
(pp. 494-95)

Stan is as isolated at this moment as he has ever been. The evangelist deserts him, and when Amy happens to come up—with the nutmeg-grater lost years before—he is still powerless to communicate his vision. As Stan then walks stiffly towards the house, his seizure coincides with a last illumination:

"What is it, Stan?" she asked.

Her face was afraid.

I believe, he said, in the cracks in the path. On which ants were massing, struggling up over an escarpment. But struggling. But joyful. So much so, he was trembling. The sky was blurred now. As he stood waiting for the flesh to be loosened on him, he prayed for greater clarity, and it became obvious as a hand. It was clear that One, and no other figure, is the answer to all sums.

"Stan," cried his wife, running, because she really was afraid that she had been left behind . . .

"It is all right," he said.

She was holding his head and looking into it some minutes after there was anything left to see. (p. 495)

There are those in *The Tree of Man* whose experience exceeds the range of Stan Parker's: Mr Gage, who hangs himself in his backyard, and Doll Quigley, who finishes her life in an asylum. The torments of the exceptional soul White is to explore in the books that follow. *The Tree of Man* deals with the plight of the common mortal, whose life is for the most part unfulfilled, whose experience is more limited, uncomprehending and laborious. If Stan cannot be the fully "representative" figure of White's epic design, his history can yet include the earnest and rather pitiful life of someone like old Armstrong the ex-butcher, as Voss's could not; he is still struggling painfully amid his relationships to other people, while Miss Hare has replaced them with relationships to goats or skeletons of leaves. It is through his bewilderment and stubbornness—its most moving aspects—that his life is most a paradigm, and what it expresses even more strongly— through his struggle to resist it—is the incurable loneliness of the soul. *The Tree of Man* may fill one with trepidation at what it sets out to do, but it stands firm on what in a rather different way it has achieved.

1/1965

The Gothic Splendours: Patrick White's *Voss*

JAMES McAULEY

The novel is usually thought of as the characteristic literary expression of the interests and values predominant in European society in the eighteenth and nineteenth centuries. It corresponds to the primacy of secular values, and the pushing of transcendental themes into the background. Within the secular sphere, it represents the turning away from the exaltation of the aristocratic values of honour, heroism and warrior prowess to a concern with class, money, marriage and everyday moral issues. Its main style of presentation is naturalistic verisimilitude, in keeping with an age whose great achievements were in empirical science with its method of detailed factual observation.

Of course, this mainstream of "bourgeois" naturalism was not unvaried, nor did it lack competing currents. Tendencies other than those enumerated above could fasten on the form and seek to mould it to different ends. In *Moby Dick* a different kind of prose fiction results from a mythopoeic impulse wrestling darkly with the material. Dostoievsky grasped the novel of his day and made it the vehicle of his prophetic intuition of the depths of the spiritual crisis of modern man. Writers like Loti made it the vehicle of a cult of romantic primitivism and exoticism. James Joyce turned it into a sort of profane liturgy of the religion of art. Lawrence tried to break through its firm conventions of character-presentation in a solid institutional setting in order to give a fiery fluid revelation of the passional depths underlying these congealed structures.

Such works as I have mentioned use more or less of the

naturalistic techniques of the novel, depending on their purpose. They are to be distinguished from the "novel proper"—which may, as modern criticism so well knows, carry potentialities for schematic or symbolic or mythopoeic sub-intention within the firm framework of its primary novelistic virtues—by the fact that an impulse from outer space has seized upon the form and is distorting its normal growth. Such works are best called meta-novels. Patrick White, in writing *Voss* revealed the growing strength of meta-novelistic ambitions in his work, which have continued into *Riders in the Chariot*. The customary procedures of novel-writing are in *Voss* subdued to an aim transcending naturalistic fiction, and where necessary the conventional code is broken arbitrarily and without discussion.

At the time of the book's appearance, I asked whether Patrick White does not fulfil in *Voss* poetic intentions of greater depth and sustained intensity than are to be found in Australian poetry. The very things that White undertakes are things which have been the normal business of poetic narrative and drama. He presents a significant action, examined in all its levels of psychological penetration, pathos, irony, moral and metaphysical meaning; and his method of telling constrains us, if we are to follow at all, to a close attention which induces a vivid and almost hallucinated response. The challenge remains to the poets whether they have not let their art fall away too easily from the greater tasks. The attempted revival of poetic drama has been one effort to recover form and scope for such an undertaking, but this has not been fully successful. I may as well confess that in my recollection there is a link between my reaction to *Voss* and my decision to write *Captain Quiros*, though the work as it actually developed does not invite further comparison.

What I want to do briefly here is to make a thematic analysis of *Voss*. This is the part of literary criticism which I find most congenial myself, and which I find most rewarding when done by others. It has its deviations and vices—for example, an uncontrolled over-interpretation of motifs; or else the using of the theme merely to hang on to it a miscellany of gleanings from the surrounding areas of cultural history, which end by stupefying rather than illuminating—but it remains the primary task in regard to all works of any pretension to intellectual and imaginative height.

In Australian literature, the Bush has figured in a too-easy contrast with the City. It is the wild against the sown, the hard school of manhood against the soft life; it is also primitive virtue against artificial corruption—all the streams issuing from eighteenth-century reveries on the subject of Natural Man flow into it.

Now, the story of *Voss* is organized in a contrast between the urban society of Sydney a century ago and the untamed unexplored Bush. And indeed the Bush functions in a set of symbolic relations. Sydney is the area of provincial gentility, of money-making, of conventional piety, and materialist incrustation; whereas in the Bush the urban concealments and compromises are torn off, and the raw visionary heart of man moves in its proper landscape. That is why, as Laura says: "Everyone is still afraid, or most of us, of this country and will not say it. We are not yet possessed of understanding."[1]

Nevertheless, in his use of the symbolic potentialities of the Bush, White transcends the too-simple contrast while giving value to the amount of truth it contains. The Bush is "the country of the mind" in which man stands unprotected before the fundamental issues, and faces the real revelations if they ever come: "Perhaps true knowledge only comes of death by torture in the country of the mind" (p. 475). But observe that Laura, who says this, and knows what it means from her own experience, fulfilled her agony in Sydney. The Bush is a symbolic region, a way of picturing an inner world that urban man, too, enters if he has the courage and metaphysical depth to explore his selfhood and his relation to God.

It is this that provides a partial answer, at least, to the complaints of knowledgeable bushmen that many details of Voss's expedition are untrue to any likelihood or possibility. One might bow to such knowledgeable rebukes without surrendering the chief value of the passages in question.

Clearly, much depends on White's ability to render the external scene in such a way as to convert it into a visionary

---

[1] *Voss* (1957), p. 31. All page references are to this edition.

landscape with figures. A remark made by White in correspondence with me, which I quote with his permission, sheds light on his own clear awareness of this, and on the manner in which he approached the task: "When I was writing *Voss* I tried to make it *look* like a Blake drawing, on the mystical, and a Delacroix on the worldly plane." The memorable scenes of the exterior-interior landscape correspond to this intention, and to the theme that is at the heart of the book:

> There was an air of peace at that camp, since rain had drowned many doubts. Thick, turbulent, yellow water was now flowing in the river bed. Green, too, was growing in intensity, as the spears of grass massed distinctly in the foreground, and a great, indeterminate green mist rolled up out of the distance. Added to the gurgle of water were the thousand pricking sounds of moist earth, the sound of cud in swollen cheeks of cattle, and sighs of ravaged horseflesh that looked at last fed and knowing. There was the good scent of rich, recent, greenish dung. Over all this scene, which was more a shimmer than the architecture of landscape, palpitated extraordinary butterflies. Nothing had been seen yet to compare with their colours, opening and closing, opening and closing. Indeed, by the addition of this pair of hinges, the world of semblance communicated with the world of dream. (p. 277)

One wonders whether it is not this metaphysical theme, far more than any incidental oddities of style, that made some local readers uneasy and resistant in the face of *Voss*, as if White were guilty of Un-Australian Activities. I am thinking not merely or mainly of published reviews, but chiefly of desultory comment in conversation. White's strategy in taking such an eminently proper line as an Australian historical theme, with exploration and all that, and then doing the thing in an anti-naturalistic way, set up contradictory responses which paralysed judgment.

The metaphysical theme emerges in a conversation between Laura and Voss. Already we have been told that Laura has given up belief in God—the God of her governesses and her aunt. "Already as a little girl she had been softly sceptical, perhaps out of boredom; she was suffocated by the fuzz of faith" (p. 11). So to Voss she says: "I do not pray" (p. 95).

"*Ach*", he pounced, "you are not *atheistisch*?"

The German word gives this a more serious and funda-

37

mental character, lifts it out of the chatter and superficiality of the Sydney environment. Voss, it turns out, disapproves of atheism. But why? Most atheists, according to him, disbelieve for mean reasons: in their own pettiness "they cannot conceive the idea of a Divine Power". But it becomes evident that Voss is really an atheist of another kind. He conceives, and believes in, "the idea of a Divine Power"; he affirms that there is a Godhead, that there is, so to speak, a Universal Throne requiring an occupant. But that occupant is not to be God the Father, nor the God-Man Christ: no, man must attain the Godhead, and seat himself as King upon that throne. He, Voss, will do it; and this is the real inner meaning of that expedition which in its outer aspect will be the conquest of a continent. What Voss is dedicated to is the self-deification of man, to be achieved in his own person, through boundless will and pride and daring.

To be God one must be a self-subsistent, self-sufficient autonomous being, dependent on no one and without weakness. A God may be kind and just, but he must need no one: he cannot love as creatures love, needing one another for completion of their incompleteness and support of their weakness. So therefore must Voss be, treating all feelings as an entangling weakness, and abhorring especially humility, because humility is essentially the confessing of one's creature weakness and dependence.

Laura sees this terrible obsessive ambition in him. She loves him, but there is also repulsion and pity for the man who despises a merely human destiny and will destroy his humanity in the act of self-deification. Almost without thinking, by a reflex action of her love, she re-assumes faith in God in order to be able to pray for Voss and save him. She knows intuitively that he who renounces love and humility is not deified but damned. So she says: "Then I will learn to pray for you." And he replies: "Oh dear, I have caught you out doubly", he laughed. "You are an Apostle of Love masquerading as an atheist for some inquisitorial purpose of your own" (p. 97).

What, then is Voss's conception of the trans-continental expedition?

Outwardly it is to be a conquest of the wilderness, like the expeditions of Eyre and Leichhardt, which will leave Voss's name for ever on the map.

But there is an essential duality. Voss speaks on one occasion of "our other journey" which is the one he takes towards the Godhead to which he aspires. This is essentially a ritual action. For only by ritual sacrifice can an identification with the divine be achieved. Hints on this subject lie frequent in the book. What White suggests subtly by symbolic means we must draw out in stark summary. Voss has made himself High Priest of a sacrifice, the aim of which is self-identification with the Godhead. Who are the chosen victims for this sacrifice? They are himself, in his merely human being, and the members of his party, in theirs. Voss's own poor daily self must suffer in the desert, be mortified, and if necessary die. The more this self-mortification and self-immolation in the desert proceeds, the more nearly will he achieve, he thinks, identification with the Godhead:

> Voss was jubilant as brass. Cymbals clapped drunkenly. Now he had forgotten words, but sang his jubilation in a cracked bass, that would not have disgraced temples, because dedicated to God.
> Yes, GOTT. He had remembered. He had sung it. It rang out, shatteringly, like a trumpet blast.
> Even the depths lead upward to that throne, meandered his inspired thoughts. He straightened his shoulders, lying back along the croup of the crazily descending horse. It had become quite clear from the man's face that he accepted his own divinity. It was less clear, he was equally convinced that all others must accept. After he had submitted himself to further trial, and, if necessary, immolation. (pp. 153-54)

And in other passages he eyes his companions as sacrificial victims—but they are merely animal sacrifices, as it were, for the deification is beyond them. Thus he sees the rich young squatter, Ralph Angus: "But Angus might prove a worthy sacrifice. The young bull of pagan rites, he would bellow and cast up his brown, stupid eyes before submitting" (p. 188). He sends the naturalist Palfreyman to his death at the hands of the blacks. Palfreyman is a Christian, and dies as an ineffectual Christ-figure, with the spear in his side (pp. 364-65). Voss thus achieves the rejection of the Christian idea of sacrifice and substitutes his own. What defeats the completion of this ritual is the revolt of the practical earthy Judd—a suggestion of Caliban is brought in here:

> The man-animal joined them and sat for a while upon the scorching bank. It was possibly this communion with the beasts that did finally rouse his bemused human intellect, for in their company he sensed the threat of the knife, never far distant from the animal throat.
> "I will not! I will not!" he cried at last, shaking his emaciated body.
> Since his own fat paddocks, not the deserts of mysticism, nor the transfiguration of Christ, are the fate of common man, he was yearning for the big breasts of his wife, that would smell of fresh-baked bread even after she had taken off her shift.
> That evening, after the canvas water-bags had been filled against an early start, and the men were picking half-heartedly at a bit of damper and dried meat, Judd approached their leader, and said:
> "Mr Voss, sir, I do not feel we are intended to go any farther. I have thought it over, and am turning back." (pp. 367-68)

In his egoism and visionary obsession the whole journey is unreal to Voss as a practical enterprise and his companions have no rights in their own being. Indeed he has told Laura (p. 74) that it would be better that he should go barefoot and alone.

Laura understands what is involved. "This expedition, Mr Voss," said Laura Trevelyan suddenly, "this expedition of yours is pure will" (p. 74).

The other who understands is the poet Le Mesurier, who finally suicides. In the Rimbaud-like prose-poems he writes in his notebook, he images the struggle that lies at the heart of the book.

These are "the Gothic splendours of death" that Voss refers to on one occasion (p. 282). "Gothic splendours" is a well chosen term, for it reminds us that Voss is a child of European Romanticism, and especially of German Romanticism in its most characteristic phases. The ambition to transcend humanity, to transfigure it and attain the level of divinity—either through action or through artistic inspiration—recurs under many masks in Romantic literature and the thinkers associated with it. Nietzsche was the heir to this Romantic ferment.

What I want to suggest here is that White has not undertaken a purely fantastic and eccentric theme, the egomania and insane will of a single individual. He is using this heightened and dramatized instance to interpret imaginatively a tension within modern civilization, perhaps the ultimate problem of that civilization. We shall see how he defines it in its fullness later.

As we have already noted, Laura dedicates herself to saving Voss from his terrible self-destructive ambition—saving him spiritually, for of the likelihood of his physical destruction she has little doubt. She takes the opposite road to his, the road to love, of humility, of sacrifice for another, and of prayer. Her own struggle will be hard, for she has in her a pride and will not unlike that of Voss.

She begins with one initial advantage. Voss has fallen in love with her. To that extent he is already weakened and confused, for to him the need for Laura's love and understanding is incompatible with the flawless hard diamond-purity of self-sufficient will which he aspires to. Voss is no longer simply on one side, as the embodiment of the demand for self-deification. He has become the battle-field in which his pride and will fight it out with the impulses to love, compassion, humility, identified with Laura. Which will win?

The novelist's problem is not, which will win; but, how to represent in action this interior struggle? How are Laura and Voss to interact in a spiritual contest while he is in central Australia and she in Sydney? In order to solve this problem, White goes beyond naturalistic verisimilitude and invites a "willing suspension of disbelief" as he shows a telepathic communion of spirits. While Voss is journeying in the inland Laura is there with him in the country of the mind. While Laura is in Sydney, taking the place of a mother for the bastard child of her dead servant Rose, she knows what is happening to Voss at least by partial intimations; and when she falls ill she is transported wholly with him to share his last days. It is a method of handling the problem that fits the background of High Romanticism from which the main theme comes, and it is justified by the meta-novelistic form and spirit of the whole work. If it were a conventional novel we should have to ask ourselves whether such an extensive clairvoyance and telepathy was sufficiently probable to gain our credence. Since it is not such a novel, we can accept it without raising the question.

From the beginning of the expedition Laura is in Voss's mind as the alternative to his self-deifying mania:

He lay thinking of the wife from whose hands he would accept salvation, if he were intended to renounce the crown of fire for the ring of gentle gold. That was the perpetual question which grappled him as coldly as iron. (p. 227)

Laura does indeed win, and the spiritual marriage of the two takes place, but not the physical. Voss's redemption comes too late to save him or his companions from the destruction which his sacrificial intention had willed them into. Perhaps this was because the agony of self-renunciation and self-sacrifice which Laura had undertaken for him was imperfect. Laura decides to give up the child Mercy to fosterparents:

"If I were to make some big sacrifice", Laura was saying. "I cannot *enough*, that is obvious, but something of a personal nature that will convince a wavering mind. If it is only human sacrifice that will convince man that he is not God." (p. 394)

But her will wavers and Mercy stays with her. She trusts to God to accept her failure "in the light of intentions" (p. 421).

However, that is looking ahead. Voss's redemption comes slowly and by stages, which are also stages of disaster. The first stage is that Voss submits to the kindly ministrations of the ex-convict Judd during an illness. Voss despises weakness and has difficulty in accepting compassion or help. He writes to Laura, in a letter that will never be delivered:

Judd is what people call a *good man*. . . . It is tempting to love such a man, but I cannot kill myself quite off, even though you would wish it, my dearest Laura. I am reserved for further struggles, to wrestle with rocks, to bleed if necessary, to ascend. Yes, I do not intend to stop short of the Throne for the pleasure of grovelling on lacerated knees in company with Judd and Palfreyman. (p. 231)

Later, when the poet Frank Le Mesurier falls ill and suffers diarrhoea, it is Voss who tends him, cleaning the nauseating filth. But the struggle goes on until the lost expedition is a hopeless remnant. Judd has led two of the party back in an attempt to regain civilization, and of these only Judd survives. Those who remain with Voss are those who have been bound by his will and have accepted him as their Lord: Le Mesurier, the poet, who understands and assents to the inner drama; the simple-minded lad Harry Robarts; and also the black boy Jackie. The blacks are closing in on them; and it is not till then that Voss finally renounces Godhead; "I am no longer your Lord, Harry" he says to the lad (p. 390). Le Mesurier asks him what is his plan. Again he renounces his role: "I have no plan," replied Voss, "but will trust to God" (p. 403). Le Mesurier is blasted to hopelessness by this admission, even though he had always known in his heart that the process of self-deification must fail. He cuts his throat and dies.

Lying wasted and weak, near death—the lad Harry now dead of hunger and exhaustion—Voss turns to the God-Man with whom he had disputed the Throne of the universe:

"*O Jesus,*" he cried, "*rette mich nur! Du lieber!*"
Of this, too, mortally frightened, of the arms, or sticks, reaching down from the eternal tree, and tears of blood, and candle-wax. Of the great legend becoming truth. (p. 415)

United now with Laura, they pass, in his visions, through a surreal symbolic landscape. A strange passage concludes this visionary journey:

All these objects of scientific interest the husband was constantly explaining to his wife, and it was quite touching to observe the interest the latter professed even when most bored. (p. 418)

This wry ironic bathos at the very climax of the novel is hard to interpret with certainty. It is somewhat in the tradition of the German Romanticism evoked by Voss; it has a kinship with the grotesque symbols just described in the visionary landscape; it recalls us suddenly to the presence of the gawky actual man Voss and the stiff, rather bluestocking young woman that Laura is; and it reinforces the vein of ambiguity, the wary avoidance of ultimate commitment on the issues involved that pervades the book.

Anyway Laura has won. Voss's ambition is to be fulfilled in the way he had rejected: through love and humility, for, as Laura sees, the Christian way is also a deification of man: God becomes man so that man shall be raised to God. Laura says to the uncomprehending doctor who is attending her in her fever: "When man is truly humbled, when he has learnt that he is not God, then he is nearest to becoming so. In the end, he may ascend" (p. 411). This corresponds to the very ancient Christian theological conception of the "divinization" or "theosis" of man.

Also, Voss is sacrificed in the wilderness after all. The blacks force Jackie to do it with the knife Voss had given him. He cuts off the head and flings it at the feet of the elders. At the same moment Laura's fever reaches its crisis and she begins to mend. "Perhaps true knowledge only comes of death by torture in the country of the mind."

A very interesting comparison can be made between *Voss* and another recent book which has engaged critical attention, Pasternak's *Dr Zhivago*. I am not yoking the two merely because they are outstanding original works which won a fashionable esteem at about the same time, and tended to be read in close proximity, but because it really is worthwhile considering them together.

Both books require the reader to accept something other than the conventions of naturalistic realism. Pasternak asks us to tolerate coincidences which are stretched impossibly far by naturalistic standards; and such a character as Evgraf, Zhivago's half-brother, is almost mythological in his enigmatic role. White, as we have seen, takes us further, compelling assent to the mental union of Voss and Laura at a distance. Both books employ the methods of symbolism with great subtlety. An interesting comparison and contrast could be made between the principal pairs, Zhivago-Lara and Voss-Laura. (The female in each case is the Jungian *anima* or the Blakean Emanation.) In pursuing his symbolic method, Pasternak does not try to produce psychologically realized characters: there are none in the book, and Zhivago and others are hardly even physically visualized. White, on the other hand, has been able to combine his symbolist intentions with the presentation of characters that are realized in some psychological depth and with great visual clarity. In this respect, I think his work is superior, because, even while wishing to allow Pasternak to handle things in his own way, we cannot but feel the vagueness of the persons to be a weakness, at least in something that can be described as a novel. Both books are very much concerned with a vision of the country they are dealing with and with its spiritual destiny. Both are full of poetic vision of landscape and natural things. Above all, both books are basically concerned with the ultimate issues of human life. Voss's original God-defying self-deifying humanism has affinities with the pretensions of the Communist system as presented in the Russian work. Both writers oppose to this Promethean hubris of pride and power a conception derived from Christianity, of man's redeemability and ascension through love and humility. Pasternak's treatment of this theme carries the weight and authority of one who has lived through Russia's "terrible years" and we cannot but feel the impress of the subject matter—for after all the Russian Revolution is one of the great crises in human history. White's subject does not have this accession of added impressiveness.

If one has a final reservation about both books, it is in the region where judgment of artistic performance and judgment of the value of the view of life presented cannot really be quite separated. In Pasternak's case, the finally depressing thing is the poverty of the ideas with which he opposes the Moloch of atheist humanism: the outright irrationalism and the gimcrack theosophy, with a Christianizing wash—ideas of 1905 which he carried incapsulated and undeveloped across the years. If this were all that could be offered as a hope and method of recovery, must one not despair? And the critique which has its roots in one's dissatisfaction with Pasternak's ideas leads back into the work, discovering how much of it is weakened and tainted by ultimate intellectual failure at the heart of the book.

In White's case, I have already spoken of the wary evasiveness with which the issues are handled—an evasiveness which increases in the last part of the book. The Christian framework is assumed in the book for the purpose of stating the issues, and up to a point for resolving them. But in the last part the framework of interpretation seems itself to slip and become unclear. The critical question is whether this ambiguity and wariness, to which the manneristic style of the book lends itself, is not also a limitation upon artistic success.

"Our relationship is ruined by interrogation," says Colonel Hebden to Laura at the end (p. 469). The problem is whether an equivocal assessment of the events, encouraged by the author, does not tend to disintegrate what he has created: and whether the kind of interrogation of the author's intention which the book invites is adequately received when the reader accepts the invitation and presses the inquiry.

1/1965

Archetypes and Stereotypes:
Riders in the Chariot

J. F. BURROWS

Among the most striking, if not altogether convincing, scenes in Patrick White's *Riders in the Chariot* (1961) is that where the Jew Himmelfarb is crucified by a sordidly xenophobic mob of workers from Rosetree's factory at Barranugli. While Rosetree, cast as Judas-Pilate, escapes from the factory-yard to the safety of his office and while Dubbo the aboriginal painter, cast as Peter, looks on in impotent horror, the mob truss Himmelfarb to a lopped jacaranda-tree. "At least one of his hands was pierced. Through the torn shirt, it could be seen that the disgraceful ribs were gashed" (p. 461). While Himmelfarb prays for a sign, a man spits in his face and a girl throws an orange—no doubt a bitter one. Though not themselves present and though lacking any natural knowledge of what is going on, the "two Marys" are portentously involved. Mrs Godbold is preparing "to lay the body in her whitest sheets" and "remembering . . . how the women . . . had received the body of their Lord" (p. 462); while "at that hour, descending the stairs at Xanadu, Miss Hare saw the marble shudder, the crack widen a little farther" (p. 461). Himmelfarb is at last cut down, and conveniently survives until after midnight, enabling Mrs Godbold to remark that "Mr Himmelfarb, too, has died on the Friday" (p. 493).

This scheme of reference has drawn the attention, usually hostile, of a number of those who have discussed the novel. Thus Margaret Walters speaks of "arbitrary Biblical parallels";[1] and Colin Roderick, who sees the whole novel as "a

---

[1] Margaret Walters, "Patrick White", *New Left Review*, 18 (January 1963), 37-50.

fictional essay in Jewish mysticism", complains of the marring of this mysticism "by the alien imposition of the central drama of Christian dogma".[2] These critics object also to the Chariot itself, chief symbol of the moments of mystical vision achieved by the four *illuminati* of the novel. To Roderick, the Chariot is to be understood strictly in terms of Kabbalism and Merkabah mysticism: it is thus a prime force in making the novel as esoteric, and therefore unconvincing, as he ultimately finds it. To Miss Walters, the Chariot is a leading example of a "factitiousness" that leads her naturally to the larger judgment that "White's attempt to re-create the Christian story never succeeds in suggesting a contemporary relevance, nor do the resonances he borrows from it really illuminate his portrayal of modern living."

Without wishing to become aligned with those who engulf the novel in a sea of vague superlatives, one must raise the possibility that, in this decidedly mythic novel, the mythic element is ultimately neither factitious nor esoteric but something essentially related to contemporary issues as explored by White. If this can be established, even the admitted failings of the novel will assume a more interesting aspect, revealing qualities more complex than the rigid and simple formulae of Roderick and Miss Walters can admit.

In the first place, the novel's reference to the Bible is much more constant than has been acknowledged. Indeed an attempt to gather together even the more explicit of its Biblical allusions leads to a result which at first looks incoherent. Within a single paragraph (p. 441), Sydney is called Sodom, Nineveh, and Babylon. Situated on its outskirts is Rosetree's factory which is at once Calvary and "the infernal pit" (p. 222). Not far away, outside Sarsaparilla, stands Miss Hare's decrepit mansion, Xanadu, which is not only the temple of Jerusalem but also an Eden or pseudo-Eden (pp. 12-13). Himmelfarb, whom we have already seen as Christ, has long been regarded by Jews of his acquaintance as a prospective Messiah. At the time of his wife's capture by the Nazis (p. 171), he is Job. His name is Mordecai, and he much resembles that upright and scholarly Jew of the Babylonian captivity who

---

[2] Colin Roderick, "*Riders in the Chariot*: an Exposition", *Southerly*, XXII, ii (1962), 62-77.

figures in the Book of Esther. When he travels from Sarsaparilla to Paradise East, on the North Shore, he is Joshua crossing the Jordan into the Promised Land (pp. 429-30). Yet his return journey is a return to "a state of bondage they had never really left" (p. 440). And again, a little before his death, he is Moses still crossing the desert: "From the fringes of Kadesch, a blue haze promised Nebo over on the right" (p. 481: cf. *Deuteronomy* xxxii, 48-51). Mrs Godbold and Miss Hare are the two Marys of the Crucifixion (p. 490) and also two of the "living creatures" of the vision of Ezekiel (p. 514). Mrs Godbold also makes an appearance as Elijah the Tishbite, the Messianic harbinger[3] (pp. 443-44), and, especially as maid to Mrs Chalmers-Robinson, is at one with her Scriptural namesake, Ruth. Miss Hare, furthermore, is not only an Eve-figure (e.g. p. 198) but also the "black but comely bride" of the Song of Solomon (pp. 101 ff., 174-75). Alf Dubbo, who is to become Peter, has been at times in his boyhood (pp. 351-74) both Moses and Joseph. And, after Himmelfarb's death, there is good reason for seeing Dubbo as that unnamed Enoch who, in *Revelation* xi, joins Elijah in bearing witness to the fall of Sodom.[4] Even the Judas-figure, the unfortunate Mr Rosetree, makes a brief appearance as Joseph of Arimathea (pp. 499-501).

A first step towards discovering the order that actually constitutes this apparent chaos is to invoke the familiar notion of point of view. All four *illuminati* see a mystical chariot which, as White acknowledges (e.g. pp. 348-50), is primarily though not exclusively drawn from the Book of Ezekiel. There, however, the initial resemblance ends: they are very different individuals springing from very different backgrounds. Easily the best educated of the four, Himmelfarb has most to tell us of his visions and, by the same token, he supplies us with most of the Old Testament allusions. Yet he must not be allowed to overwhelm our understanding.

---

[3] Cf. *The Passover Haggadah*, tr. Cecil Roth (Soncino Press, 1934), p. xii, p. 54. Here and elsewhere I am indebted to Dr A. D. Crown, of the University of Sydney, for directing me to leading experts and important documents in a field new to me.

[4] Cf. Louis Ginzberg, *The Legends of the Jews* (Philadelphia, Jewish Publication Society, 1909-28), i. 125-40; v. 157.

Where their beliefs differ significantly from Himmelfarb's, we must attend also to the naive but grandiose Gospel-faith of Mrs Godbold, to the assimilation of *Ezekiel, John,* and *Revelation* which Dubbo at last achieves, and to the Blakean pantheism of Miss Hare. We must therefore expect diverse accounts of any crucial scene in which more than one of the *illuminati*, not to mention the unilluminated, take part.

Dubbo is chiefly responsible for the Christian account of the Crucifixion-episode, the only account to which critics of the novel have attended. To Himmelfarb the scene is Messianic indeed, but by no means Christian. The sense of mission that has haunted him all his life has gradually become one with his need to atone for his betrayal to Sammaël (Satan) of his wife and, as he believes, his people. Events have forced on him the reluctant belief that he may indeed be the Messiah. Fearful of arrogance but driven by the need to atone, Himmelfarb assumes the Messianic rôle of the "suffering servant" (cf. *Isaiah* lii-liii). Thus inspired, he is able to achieve and maintain, throughout the "crucifixion", a mood of serenity quite distinct from the resignation giving place to despair ("Eli, Eli . . .") of Christ's Passion. It is only *after* his rescue that Himmelfarb despairs. Then he is desolate because "it had not been accorded to him to expiate the sins of the world" (p. 469; cf. p. 479). Meanwhile White takes pains to diminish any implication of a morbid luxuriance. Thus, in the moment of Himmelfarb's spiritual desolation, "the pulses of his body expressed gratitude for the resolved situation in which he found himself so simply and so naturally placed" (p. 469).

In the Crucifixion-episode, it emerges, White is seeking to express at once the Judaism of Himmelfarb, the revived Christianity of Dubbo, the grinding tension between Judaism and Christianity that is destroying Rosetree, and the xenophobia of the Sarsaparillan mob. The full complexity of the attempt appears only in the text itself; but something of it can be epitomized in two tiny details. The truncated jacaranda-tree is an apt enough symbol of the Sarsaparillan ugliness. For Dubbo, it comes to symbolize not only the Cross but also the purple robe of Christ. To Himmelfarb, however, it symbolizes the sacred blue of Israel, the colour of the Celestial Throne and the colour, I take it, here signified by the name "Himmelfarb" itself. (It is also the colour of the hands of Israel the dyer who, long before, had set Himmelfarb on paths that were to lead him to this Tree.) Similarly, the sheets prepared by Mrs Godbold for her Lord represent also the contempt in which this washerwoman is held by the worthies of Sarsaparilla. For Himmelfarb, in the moment of his death, they assume the form of the *kittel*, that ceremonial shawl which symbolizes, among other things, reunion with his own past and with his lost wife, Reha, and also "man's final deliverance from human bondage and from human misery".[5]

Notwithstanding the ironies (pp. 453-55) through which White seeks to relieve its more extravagant overtones, there is undoubtedly an air of strain about this episode. And yet it is no crude straining after merely spectacular effects. Rather is it the mark of a somewhat laboured attempt to achieve a complex juxtaposition of sharply different attitudes. Both *The Man who Died* and *Light in August* show that there have been novelists who could carry off an analogous scene with less sign of effort. Among novelists of the present time, however, it is difficult to think of anyone else who would know how to begin. There is something a little unreasonable about the critic who bases firm-sounding judgments of such a scene on a demonstrably superficial reading of it.

Nor do the complexities of this or other scenes require any very erudite unravelling. Granted the unremarkable step of expecting a fervent Jew to think in Messianic rather than Christian terms, the rest emerges clearly enough from the text itself. It is here that Roderick's erudite commentary is misleading. Although the Jewish mysticism which he expounds (and which he does not distinguish sufficiently from the more esoteric but less relevant Kabbalah)[6] is indeed a force in the novel, it is not the only force and, with rare and trivial exceptions, it is *in* the novel. For most of us, the identity of Adam Kadmon, who descends "from the Tree of Light to take the Bride" (p. 483), needs to be sought in reference-books. But ignorance of Adam Kadmon's precise

---

[5] *The Passover Haggadah* (tr. Roth), pp. xi-xii.
[6] See, for example, C. D. Ginsburg, *"The Essenes" & "The Kabbalah": Two Essays (Routledge*, 1863-4, re-published 1955), p. 226.

identity need not inhibit a precise awareness of the emotional
significance of Himmelfarb's visionary reunion with Reha—
especially when, in direct contrast to their earthly wedding
long before (p. 141), he and Reha "did not break the cup, as
the wedding guests expected, but took and drank, again and
again" (p. 483). Similarly, it is true that Mrs Godbold's hymn
about the Chariot (p. 257) is, as Roderick says, "the Bishop
of Lincoln's paraphrase of Daniel's Kabbalistic verse". It is
much more pertinent that this is a famous Christian hymn,
sung here by an ardent Christian who knows nothing of
Judaism, much less Kabbalism. And, finally, Elijah's rôle on
the Passover Night rests upon a belief that has been incor-
porated in the Passover ceremony for over two thousand
years. The argument that this "fictional essay in Jewish mysticism" is too esoteric to be relevant to our society, decries a
state of affairs that the critic, rather than White, has created.

Granted, then, that it is only others who see Himmelfarb
as Christ, it remains true that Himmelfarb sees himself as
Moses, Joshua, Mordecai, and so on. This "contradictoriness"
of reference is a barrier only to the literal-minded. What is
called for is a flexible approach akin to that of Biblical
typology. To read such a work as Ginzberg's *Legends of the
Jews* or to dabble in either rabbinical or patristic commen-
taries on the Bible is, for me at least, to be impressed above
all by the way in which almost every character or event is
interpreted as a looking forward to or a looking back upon
other characters and other events. The part played by Enoch
in *Genesis* is brief and, on the face of it, unimportant. Yet
the commentators identify prophet after prophet throughout
the Old Testament as avatars of Enoch; and, even in *Revelation*, it is "Enoch" who, with "Elijah", bears witness to the
fall of "Sodom". In a context of Biblical myth, especially as
seen by a Himmelfarb, a shifting back and forth between
Adam and Moses, Elijah, Mordecai, and Job is no matter for
wonder or dismay but simply an inevitability.[7] Setting aside
all such merely literal paradoxes, let us consider Himmelfarb's career as an attempt to redeem Israel.

[7] Cf. Northrop Frye, *Anatomy of Criticism* (Princeton, 1957), p. 315. Elsewhere (e.g. pp. 191-3) Frye's remarks are more pertinent still to *Riders in the
Chariot*.

The explicit identification, mentioned earlier, of Himmelfarb with the Messiah and of his sense of mission with the fate of Israel begins in his boyhood when a Galician rabbi searches his forehead for a Messianic sign (p. 108). It continues in his relationship with Israel the dyer (e.g. pp. 121, 142-43) and with his own wife (p. 214). He is insistently seen, furthermore, as a scapegoat and as the ram in the thicket which so obligingly took Isaac's place beneath Abraham's knife (pp. 124-25, 169, 215). Germany is never actually called Egypt, but it is explicitly seen (pp. 159-60) as a place where Israel is in bondage, and Himmelfarb's father is led from the paths of righteousness by its flesh-pots and by the golden calf which here is Christianity. Even Konrad Stauffer, that representative of the German conscience, falls into place as a kindly Egyptian, whether Potiphar or Joseph's Pharaoh. After Reha's disappearance, Himmelfarb surrenders to the Nazis, who are seen as Sammaël incarnate (p. 161), and begins his attempt to make atonement. The distinctly Kabbalistic Chariot of his earlier intellectuality (p. 151) becomes now (p. 190) and hereafter a Chariot of Redemption, a sign more "simply" mystical: as he himself later remarks, "The intellect has failed us" (p. 221). His first active endeavour to redeem his people takes place on the journey to the concentration-camp of Friedensdorf. In a brilliantly-wrought passage (pp. 200-05), his failure is marked by his growing recognition of the monstrous reality that lies behind the innocent appearance of Friedensdorf itself: what had seemed a Paradise proves to be one of the most terrible deserts of all. After a miraculous escape from this Egyptian bondage and after further wanderings in a desert that is now chiefly psychological, he comes to Palestine. For him, however, Palestine is not the Promised Land. Guided by a "very definite pillar of fire" (p. 216), his journey continues until he reaches Sydney. Here, in Babylon, he finds himself a house like Mordecai's, a small house hidden among willows. Here he is to experience a strange and complex relationship (to which we shall return) with that sufficiently black but none too comely bride, Miss Hare. Here he is to achieve, in his getting of wisdom and in the manner of his dying, a Messianic apotheosis bearing with it, for some minds, a redemptive power.

But Mordecai Himmelfarb is no more the author of *Riders in the Chariot* than of its Crucifixion-scene. Even in "his" narrative, his account of things seldom goes unchallenged, whether by another character or by the impersonal narrator. Often the challenge to Himmelfarb's myth is quite unmythic: this quasi-Messiah is also a "bloody reffo". Often, again, Himmelfarb's myth is challenged by a myth of another provenance. It is the narrator who supplies Orphic resonances when Reha (pp. 170-71) and the Lady from Czernowitz (p. 205) recede into the darkness while a Job-like Himmelfarb vainly and desolately calls after them. And Orpheus is in the background once again when the Jew, torn in what had begun as a Bacchanal (pp. 454-57), drifts from Rosetree's factory-yard "with the gentle, uncertain motion of an egg-shell tossed by flowing water" (p. 469).

This juxtaposing of disparate conceptions of things is not, of course, confined to scenes in which Himmelfarb is protagonist. There are moments when Mrs Flack, chief inspiration of those evil forces which conspire against him, is an incarnate Satan. More characteristically, however, her provenance is classical. It is presumably in Delphic terms that we are to understand her being "priestess" and "pythoness"; her leading of the incantations in which that "adept" Mrs Jolley shares as inwardly she "crouched before the tripod" (p. 251); and her "need for invocation before encounter with superior powers" (p. 444). In the same way, there are occasions when the Biblical Dubbo gives place to a Prometheus-figure, less disposed to the ascending fire of apotheosis than to the bringing down of the fires of inspiration, and afterwards tormented by parrots whose "playful beaks, would have entered, and sat picking, inside his cage of ribs" (p. 512).

From the evidence so far considered it emerges that the mythic parallels of the novel are more formidable and wide-ranging than Roderick and Miss Walters, in their different ways, suggest. It emerges, too, that these parallels are ordered in terms of "point of view" and that, partly by their aid, the novel is marked by a juxtaposing of radically different points of view. A study of Dubbo's career should advance our inquiry a further stage.

For most of his life, Alf Dubbo is an alien in his own land, the victim of a country rector's Great Experiment in assimilation. The chief effect of this experiment is to establish in Dubbo a bitter and enduring conflict between different conceptions of life, love, and art. In part Dubbo's problem is racial. His difficulties nevertheless stem less from racial alienation—of his native culture only scattered intensities survive in him—than from his inability to resolve the contradictions of white society itself. The rector preaches a gospel of Love according to St John—and seduces the boy. The rector's sister preaches that "art is first and foremost a moral force" (p. 355) —but prefers "to avert her eyes from nature" (p. 354), not to speak of the boy's too honest paintings. It is in a half-calculating desire to please her that the boy, betraying himself, makes an abortive attempt at painting Christ. Long after he has left the rectory, Dubbo is still trying to resolve the conflict between "woolly precepts of God in cloud and God in man" (p. 374) and the actualities of grog, syphilis, the betrayal of his vocation, and an unending line of meaningless tasks. He cannot, even in this period, suppress his creative impulse: but his chief progress is in the aridities of "technique"; and the "chariot-thing" that has long haunted his imagination does not—indeed cannot—advance beyond a preliminary cartoon.

Woolly as its precepts seem to him, Dubbo draws constantly on the Bible, his only substantial store of imaginative riches. It is in predominantly Biblical terms, therefore, that he struggles to understand and express himself and his society, as when his sense of calling and his hatred for "Babylon" are realized in a painting of the Lord's Elect, engulfed but not consumed by the fiery furnace of Nebuchadnezzar. Indeed his whole career, so far as its tensions allow form at all, assumes the form of a Biblical myth, analogous to but more specifically Christian than Himmelfarb's. Meanwhile the narrator keeps the strictly artistic aspect of this career before us by means of occasional Promethean touches.

Dubbo's conception of the Chariot is renewed when he comes upon the Chariot-vision of Ezekiel, and still further intensified when he discovers that *Ezekiel* means much to Himmelfarb. When Himmelfarb is crucified, Dubbo cannot bring himself to act. But, in Himmelfarb's death, the rector's precepts come to life. After the fashion expounded by Durkheim,[8] Dubbo finds self-knowledge in and redemption through "the love of the brethren". Through an awakened compassion, his understanding is enriched and the whole of his experience is reconciled. In a blaze of creative energy Dubbo paints the Deposition of Christ, thus transmuting his boyish conflicts and hypocrisies, and the Chariot, thus fusing his later experience into one vision. He dies—and his paintings are lost.

Far from being a factitious imposition on Dubbo's career, his myths *are* his career. Through them and only through them does Dubbo come to a full understanding of himself and his vocation, of his communion with Himmelfarb, of his alienation from a contemptible society, and, at last, of his need to sink that alienation in understanding and compassion.

Dubbo's success in fusing actuality and myth, and White's success in portraying that fusion, appear in the account of Dubbo's last days (pp. 506-15). Here White depends in part upon the establishing of a multitude of particulars: in glorifying Mrs Godbold as the First Mary, Dubbo does not allow her to dissolve into the faintly ethereal but takes pains to represent "the dust on her blunt shoes, the exact bulge below the armpit as she leaned forward" (p. 510); from an irresistible impulse "Dubbo portrayed the Christ darker than convention would have approved" (p. 511); the Chariot-horses "could have been rough brumbies" (p. 514); and, for Himmelfarb, the Crown of Thorns became "a crown of barbed wire" (p. 514). By means of many sensitive insights into the mind of the artist at work, White further reinforces Dubbo's credit: here he is dangerously involved, there he achieves a proper distance; here his vanity is flattered, there he is awed by a half-accidental felicity; here form discovers meaning, there meaning issues a peremptory demand for form. And only when it is over does he become aware of his utter exhaustion.

Turning, however, from scattered particulars to a single passage, let us examine part of Dubbo's portrayal of Miss Hare as the Second Mary:

So he painted her hands like the curled, hairy crooks of ferns. He painted the Second Mary curled, like a ring-tail possum, in a

[8] Cf. Maud Bodkin, *Archetypal Patterns in Poetry* (1934), pp. 277-79.

dream-time womb of transparent skin, or at centre of a whorl of faintly perceptible wind. As he worked, his memory re-enacted the trustful attitudes of many oblivious animals: drinking, scratching or biting at their own fur, abandoning themselves to grass and sun. (pp. 510-11)

So far as the painter himself is concerned, there is first his precise attention to such actualities—his boyhood revived in his lonely wanderings around Xanadu—as the "curled, hairy crooks of ferns" and the relaxed air of the "oblivious animals". Then there is the influence of Dubbo's myths: the Second Mary, a fragment of the Dreamtime, and a faint image of Ezekiel's whirlwind. Actuality and myth converge in Dubbo's conception of Miss Hare. The broad propriety of possums and crooks of fern as images for that bush-creature is obvious. At first sight, however, the air of security, even serenity, about "curled", "trustful", the sheltering womb, and the centre of that whirlwind is as grotesquely inappropriate to Miss Hare at this time as to the Second Mary at the time of the Crucifixion. But such a reading is inept. The painting is of the *deposition*, and Miss Hare is portrayed not in her earlier dismay or ensuing frenzy but in the serenity she attains beside Himmelfarb's deathbed when Dubbo, looking on, had conceived this picture (pp. 489-90). Since Dubbo's own emotions at that time had been closely akin to Miss Hare's, it is clear that a fusion of experience has occurred, that painter and picture have become inseparable.

All this is not to deny that there are some literary failings in Dubbo's artistic success. Clearly it is not that this Biblical aborigine is *ipso facto* an unconvincing hybrid. Rather is it that White's treatment at times allows the convincingly alienated artist he has created to be blurred by a stereotype of the Alienated Artist, a figure to whom White the novelist (which is not to say White the man) responds intensely but who is not, and presumably cannot be, explored in any depth. There are no garrets in Babylon—but Dubbo does his best to turn Babylon into a Montmartre of which he has never heard. As one watches him coughing his lungs out while painting his heart out, one is too sharply reminded of Hollywood's Chopin to think of the high incidence of tuberculosis among aborigines. Most troubling of all, since Lawrence has a potency that can make his influence pernicious, is the occasional excursus into bad Lawrence, as when we are offered a Lawrentian polarizing of a character who, more usually, is far too subtle and complex for that procrustean bed:

> They were the two poles, the negative and positive of his being: the furtive, destroying sickness, and the almost as furtive, but regenerating, creative act. (pp. 383-84)

And yet the total effect of this intrusive stereotype, as of the straining for unearned effect that goes with it, is not to obliterate Dubbo's individuality but only to blur an occasional edge.

Dubbo's career displays, in miniature, some leading characteristics of the novel as a whole. As social outcast he is one of several poignant representatives of the state of alienation and the trials of assimilation around which, in my view, the novel chiefly revolves. Although alienation is no new thing, it is a condition evident enough in modern society—and more evident in White's account of that society than Roderick's Kabbalistic exercises can permit him to recognize. The novel's analysis of the relationships between society and its alien inhabitants is severely flawed by the failure, yet to be considered, of the social—that is, Sarsaparillan—term in these relationships. White nevertheless offers sensitive analysis of what it is to be alien: one thinks not only of what we have seen in Dubbo but of what remains to be seen in Himmelfarb, Miss Hare, and the Rosetrees; one thinks also, though ironically, of Norbert Hare and the Xanadu he sought to create. Again and again, the better passages testify to our need to recognize but accept each other's individuality whether social, religious, or merely idiosyncratic—to recognize that men neither are nor should be so alike as to be indistinguishable. The virtues of accepting men in their individuality are never more plain than in those closing passages where, against its own better judgments, the novel endorses Mrs Godbold's obliteration of all individuality in a vague and doctrinaire loving-kindness.

Since White's aliens are individuals, in many ways as far from each other as from the Sarsaparillans, it is idle to censure the novel for its failure to display a complete *rapprochement* between them or an ultimate integration of their several myths. Their paths converge, and some valuable liaisons are achieved. But if, in one sense, the Chariot signifies these interrelationships, the surviving differences between one Chariot and another testify to that surviving individuality which we have seen instanced in Dubbo's and Himmelfarb's different conceptions of the Crucifixion. And if each of the Riders is intended to achieve a fusion of reality and myth (a fusion that is seriously defective only in Mrs Godbold and her *alter ego*, Mrs Flack—in both of whom White's failure is so gross as to warrant the application of Miss Walters' insensitive formula), it is for each of them the fusion of an individualistic conception of reality and a personally-interpreted myth. And if, finally, each of them is redeemed "through the love of the brethren", this is not to say that each must *become* his brother.

There is, again, something characteristic about those lapses into the stereotyped that mar White's portrayal of Dubbo. But whereas the stereotype of the Alienated Artist has a history of a century or more, the stereotype that brings about some other failures is of a specifically contemporary kind. The chief myths of the novel are all among those deep-rooted Western myths which, in the rather woolly literary psychology of C. G. Jung, assume the status of archetypal images. Whatever one's view of the place of archetypes in older literature, Jung himself and such disciples as Maud Bodkin[9] have influenced much contemporary writing in a special way. For the well-read writer of our time, an inevitably conscious recourse to archetypal imagery can become a valuable means of exploring relationships between traditional values and modern life; equally it can degenerate into a portentous and stereotyped allusiveness. As we shall see, the difference between Miss Hare and the later Mrs Godbold is that whereas Miss Hare is a human being whose portrayal gains in subtlety and

---

[9] A number of remarkable parallels between *Riders in the Chariot* and Miss Bodkin's *Archetypal Patterns in Poetry* (1934) suggest that White has known this particular book. But even if this is not so, his myths carry strong, sometimes blatant, Jungian overtones.

dramatic significance from subdued echoes of Eve, the later Mrs Godbold is a Magna Mater almost pure and thoroughly simple.

A third kind of stereotype, one of White's own making, is responsible for the failure of the Sarsaparillan episodes. As the main representation of the society in which the *illuminati* are set and in which they seek to discover themselves, Sarsaparilla—by intention at least, is an important dimension of *Riders in the Chariot*. But, as I have argued elsewhere,[10] White's satirical analysis of suburban values usually degenerates into a series of automatic gestures. The well-meaning Ernie Theobalds is a minor success, Mrs Jolley catches at an aspect of suburbia, and Mrs Flack will need to be discussed. More typical, however, are the cheap and repetitive gibes about false teeth, plastic, "personal towels", and the track that the Council had begun to call an avenue. And from these gibes, it is too short a step to the hysterics about Sydney at night (pp. 439-41)—hysterics that are only crudely related to Himmelfarb's distress at the time. In consequence, it becomes difficult to take the social dimension of the novel seriously and impossible to distinguish in it any precise significance.

It is through Xanadu, then, rather than through their own inherent significance, that the Sarsaparillan episodes are even loosely drawn into the mythic design of the novel. The mythic function of Xanadu is by no means straightforward, for its most obvious aspect, the echoing of *Kubla Khan*, turns out to be ironical. Through Norbert Hare, it emerges, White is subjecting to an ironic scrutiny the arbitrary exercise of that very mythologizing of everyday reality which occupies so much of this novel's attention. In Xanadu there is a stately pleasure-dome, there are "gardens . . . where blossomed many an incense-bearing tree", and there are sunny spots of greenery. But there is neither a fountain nor a sacred river—not even, indeed, a sinuous rill. And it would be naïve to regard the dark and icy cistern in which Norbert Hare drowns as a simple equivalent of Coleridge's caves of ice. The same is true of the rapt visionary and the Abyssinian maid:[11] at most they add a

---

[10] "The Short Stories of Patrick White", *Southerly*, XXIV (1964), 116-25.

[11] As in *The Aunt's Story* (1948), White has long seen Abyssinia as both admirable and significant. It is therefore tempting to regard Miss Hare as

faint resonance to Dubbo and Miss Hare. One soon recognizes that it is not White but Norbert Hare who is absorbedly imitating Coleridge and that Xanadu is a fine specimen of the ironic control that White can at times achieve.

The narrator quietly but persistently undermines Norbert's attitude to his creation:

His Pleasure Dome, *he called it*, his Xanadu, and recited the *appropriate verses* to *lady* guests as they strolled in their veils and the afternoon, inspecting the *freshly-laid* foundations of *porous* yellow stone (p. 15; my italics).

Around the house are groves of "rather unhappy exotic trees" and

necklaces of rosebeds (the *complexions* of the blooms themselves protected by little *parasols*, which occupied practically the whole of the second gardener's time) . . . (p. 21; my italics).

Although White once or twice forgets himself, only Norbert consistently endorses this alien intrusion of a sterile dilettantism. Only Norbert can overlook the "native cynicism" of the "grey raggedy scrub" which "immediately began to tangle with Norbert Hare's wilfully-created park" (p. 16). Only Norbert, in short, can believe that a true Xanadu can be created by an arbitrary act of the will, in the complete absence of any fountain of life and in a *fin-de-siècle* attempt to ignore the icy caverns, measureless to man, that for ever lie beneath —or within us. Not that his enterprise can succeed: it is in the sufficiently dark and icy, however artificial, cistern of his own Xanadu that he is at last to drown.

The wild and tumbledown beauty of Xanadu in its decline is another thing entirely. The house itself continues beautiful only in the eyes of Miss Hare, by now its sole inhabitant. At our first sight of the house in its decay, the point of view adopted is only ostensibly hers and the language carries impli-

---

"an Abyssinian maid" and to further the argument by adopting Roderick's suggestion that the Ethiopic Book of Enoch is among the chief mystical sources of the novel. The fact is, however, that the resemblances between the novel and *Enoch* are few, general, and in each case outweighed by corresponding Biblical passages, notably those that the novel quotes from *Ezekiel*. Any Ethiopic elements in Xanadu seem rather to be Coleridge's: see J. L. Lowes, *The Road to Xanadu* (1927), ch. xix.

cations necessary to the understanding of later and varied ironies:

Certainly the grass appeared *a bit neglected*, but the eyes, and not necessarily the eyes of a lover, were invariably *transfixed* by their first glimpse of Xanadu. Miss Hare herself had almost *crumbled* as she stood to watch *her vision form* (p. 18; my italics).

The garden meanwhile has attained a tangled and overgrown but quite genuine beauty, a union of the grey raggedy scrub with the surviving and assimilated vestiges of Norbert's exotic park. On the subject of the house, Himmelfarb (p. 338) and Mrs Godbold (p. 71) are more or less at one with Mrs Jolley (pp. 45-46); but only Mrs Jolley, Proserpine of the window-box, is unable to see the beauty of the garden. *Her* eye is only for the weeds: "A good thing I put me lisle stockings on" (p. 45). It is Miss Hare who chiefly admires the garden, but her joy in it is shared by Himmelfarb (p. 98) and by the wild and innocent Godbold girls (e.g. pp. 68, 71).

On one level this transforming of the garden is a triumph in White's naturalistic mode. Yet it represents also the mythic transmutation of a false Xanadu into a genuine Eden. From *Kubla Khan* we are carried back to *Paradise Lost*, one of Coleridge's chief sources. The most relevant passages (*Paradise Lost*, IV, 131-60, 173-84)—adjoining those on which Coleridge draws—concern the approach of Satan to Eden up "that steep savage Hill" until he finds his way blocked:

> so thick entwin'd,
> As one continu'd brake, the undergrowth
> Of shrubs and tangling bushes had perplext
> All path of Man or Beast that passd that way.

Since "One Gate there onely was", and that on the other side of the Garden, Satan contemptuously leaps the obstacles and lands within. Both the overgrown, almost trackless hillside and the distant, unused official gate figures in White's account of the approach to Xanadu (p. 13). More striking yet is the relationship between the "abrupt terraces" of the approach to Xanadu, with its tiers of trees whose height dizzies those who stare "too long upward at their scintillating crowns (pp. 12-13), and Milton's famous account of the forests encircling Eden:

> and over head up grew
> Insuperable highth of loftiest shade,
> Cedar, and Pine, and Firr, and branching Palm,
> A Silvan Scene, and as the ranks ascend
> Shade above shade, a woodie Theatre
> Of stateliest view. Yet higher than thir tops
> The verdurous Wall of Paradise up sprung.

To understand the part this Eden plays in the novel as a whole, we must also take into account its denizens: the twin but opposed angels who haunt its environs, and the Eve-figure who dwells lonely there until the coming of the Adamic Himmelfarb.

Squat, red, and ugly as she is in childhood, Mary Hare arouses in her dilettante father little but repugnance. In her self-absorbed and convention-ridden mother, a similar repugnance is hardly concealed by over-conscious attempts to concoct affection where none is felt. Nor is either parent much pleased by her habit of telling blunt truths. Brought up almost without companions, she becomes shy of people to the point of terror but finds solitary joy in the life of the bush around Xanadu. Her only communion with her father consists in her love for Xanadu, focused above all in a crystal chandelier and the mosaic goat of the bathroom floor. They do also briefly share an early half-vision of the Chariot, an experience both ecstatic and painful: although her father for once accepts her, he does so much as he would accept a dog. There shortly follow the visit of her English cousin, Eustace Cleugh, and the ball at Xanadu, her mother's one essay at matchmaking.

On this traumatic occasion, many things come to a head. Her doglike affection for her father transfers itself to Eustace. Her repressed sexuality is displaced into a bitter and enduring hatred of a virtual stranger, the beautiful Helen Antill, whose peacock fan and dress embroidered with tiny mirrors live in her memory. The troubled union of admiration and hatred that she feels for her mother here acquires its point of reference, in her mother's flamingo fan. Only after this night and after Norbert's ostentatious destruction of the chandelier must she be seen as mad.

When her father drowns (pp. 62-63), she is somehow implicated. The point here is not that White "dishonestly" conceals crucial facts about the extent of her guilt, but that he underplays distracting questions of fact in order to emphasize her morbid *consciousness* of guilt, a consciousness on which Mrs Jolley, afterwards her housekeeper and the disciple of Mrs Flack, is able to play. After Norbert's death she is terrified of the Chariot, for the blind fits of rage it invokes in her overwhelm her compassionate but unsentimental kinship with nature and culminate in murderous orgies. In the most hideous of these (pp. 56-57), Miss Hare incinerates a beloved pet goat that has been associated in the back of her mind with her father himself and with the black goat of the mosaic. Goaded by Mrs Jolley, who has gradually pieced these earlier happenings together, she torments herself with questions about the meaning of evil and the extent of her guilt, questions which, even at her sanest, she would have been too inarticulate to face.

At this point (pp. 98-99) Himmelfarb appears, trespassing in her orchard for the solace of a plum-tree in full blossom. The tree itself, his strange appearance, and his willingness to accept her all conspire to overcome her shyness: " . . . they stooped to negotiate the branches which were to provide their canopy" (p. 99).

In the strange and complex relationship that evolves between them, the needs of each are met by finding their complement. For her, the relationship comes to signify a resolution of her personal guilt through his willingness to become a scapegoat—she is at last to risk death in his blazing hut in an attempt to save *him* from incineration; a resolution of her more general puzzlings about evil through the influence of his educated intelligence and through her recognition that her experience of evil is insignificant compared to his; a resolution of her repressed sexuality through his willingness to accept, without any overtly sexual response, her shy eroticism; and, above all, a discovery of her own humanity in his willingness to regard her as a person rather than a spaniel. On his side, she can and does afford him an acceptance of death as natural and inevitable; a means of atoning for Reha; and, again above all, a simple acceptance of him as a human being. This "merely human relationship" is important to her for reasons already adumbrated. To him, too, it represents something in which he has never previously shared, since he has always been regarded either as super-human, a potential Messiah, or as sub-human, a dirty Jew. Even those Gentile women who had treated him "well" had not valued him as a person but merely for the allegedly exotic sexuality of the Jew. (Not that Miss Hare overlooks his being a "very ugly man, and strange": the point is that she accepts him in his own right.) If the ability of others to accept Himmelfarb has always been marred by their seeing him in terms of one preconception or another, he in turn has always been too arrogant, diffident, and self-absorbed to accept even Reha for herself. All of these complexities are present in the superbly controlled account of their second meeting (pp. 335-45).

The subdued echoes of Eden form an integral part of this conception. They are clearest in the very early account of Xanadu itself, where they confer an unstrained sense of universality and of flawed beauty. In the account of Miss Hare's early life they are very subdued indeed but are necessary to sustain our awareness that she is a woman as well as a dirty and ugly madwoman. On Himmelfarb's arrival these echoes grow stronger because he makes them so. As he appears in the novel as a whole, Himmelfarb would have been incapable of appreciating Miss Hare's plum-tree without seeing in it a Tree of Life. Nor could he have accepted her as a woman unless he had begun by seeing her as Eve or Solomon's Bride. The achievement that finally makes him human is his transcending, if only briefly and only in this one relationship, of his flair for Biblical typology. From this point on, however, his myths and his actualities are related in a new and more evenly-balanced way.

Unfortunately, the most striking characteristic of Mrs Flack and Mrs Godbold, the "angels" of this Eden, is the failure in each of them of the relationship between myth and actuality that White manages so skilfully elsewhere.

In her passive moments, admiring her "pastel-blue plastic dressing-table set" (p. 82) or listening to her stomach "rumbling liquidly" beyond her false teeth, Mrs Flack embodies all that is stereotyped about White's Sarsaparilla. In its unremitting frenzy, therefore, her xenophobia is not only an inconsistency in her but an absurd contradiction of her status as the natural product of a society so empty and aimless, so little attached even to xenophobia. Ernie Theobald's puzzled and suspicious dealings with Himmelfarb, a confused mingling of a vague wish to be kind and an unintended callousness, are much more in keeping with that society.

White's attempts to give special motives to Mrs Flack by saddling her with the blame for her husband's death and with an illegitimate son do not help matters. Potentially these are adequate motives: starved as she is of admissible sexuality, she makes Himmelfarb her victim when she learns of his quasi-sexual relations with Miss Hare and Mrs Godbold. But if these motives were meant to be significant, they should not have been left, save for sporadic hints, until very near the end when they suddenly become a melodramatic revelation of Mrs Flack's Awful Secret. And if this special motivation were successful it would still be detrimental to the novel as a whole: for such frigid and inverted sexuality in the arch-conspirator would divorce her utterly from the casual, though mealy-mouthed, promiscuity of Sarsaparilla, thus reducing the novel's social attitudes to a display of Himmelfarb's sheer bad luck in meeting so unusual a woman.

Freed of these confusions, the diabolic element in Mrs Flack might conceivably have offered a quite different but adequate basis for her function in the novel. As a figure of the Evil Mother, diametrically opposed but complementary to the Good Mother, this Mrs Flack, out of her own "motiveless malignity", might well have employed a morally obtuse Sarsaparilla as her instrument for destroying the Charioteers. Certainly Blue and Sarsaparilla are morally obtuse. But Mrs Flack's employment of them stems too much from her inadequate private motivation. Whereas the private motives of Iago, inadequate as they are, are shown to be the mere rationalization of his own puzzled attempts to understand himself, it is the narrator who offers us the private motives of Mrs Flack. And though we are not shown how Iago came to be the devil incarnate, we are powerfully shown what it is to be the devil incarnate. The display of Mrs Flack in this role consists in Delphic and Satanic resonances in the narrator's account of her uncomfortably juxtaposed with the stereotyped figure of a Sarsaparillan gossip.

As an effective force in the novel, Mrs Godbold is destroyed by an analogous disjunction between humanity and divinity. Although there are traces of both elements throughout, she represents less the uneasy coexistence of humanity and divinity than an arbitrary and radical change through which her divinity overwhelms her humanity.

If we set aside her vision in the cathedral (p. 265)—an experience that she finds moving rather than comprehensible—and a few smaller hints of her ultimate apotheosis, the young Ruth Joyner represents White's gift for ironic Freudianism at its best. Along with her benevolence, there are insistent reminders of her clumsiness, of her stupidity, and in one or two important passages (e.g. pp. 293-95) of the deep clash in her between a natural and generous sexuality and a self-imposed cult of chastity. More important, we are shown, with a masterly irony, how her lust for vicarious motherhood, which overpowers anyone unwary enough to stay within reach, stems from her relationship with her widowed father, from the horrible death of a younger brother whom it was her duty to "mother", and from her deep sense of rejection when her father marries again. Tom Godbold, who is to become her husband-son, speaks for the novel to this point when he abuses her for acting "Like somebody's bleedin' mother!" (p. 292). Under all the circumstances his later brutality may arouse fellow-feeling rather than disgust. All these threads are drawn together when she sets out to "rescue" him from Mrs Khalil's brothel. There, unfortunately, she learns that even whores have hearts and, through an encounter with Dubbo, that even aboriginals can be mothered. Unfortunately—because thereafter the ironies drop away and Mrs Godbold begins to be endorsed as a Magna Mater, bounteous source of the milk of loving-kindness that floods the last chapters of the novel.

The most disturbing aspect of this arbitrary and radical change in Mrs Godbold is that, in the woman herself, there is no change worth mentioning. The change that matters is in the attitude of the narrator. Up to the brothel-episode Mrs Godbold's overwhelming rage for motherhood is subjected to a robust, though carefully-qualified irony seldom found in White's work. (Miss Docker, in *A Cheery Soul,* is a magnificent exception.) Thereafter, almost without warning and on no substantial ground, the narrator proceeds to canonize her. Consider, for instance, the fate of the luckless Harry Rosetree.

As his change of name from Haïm Rosenbaum implies, Rosetree goes through all the motions of assimilation, showing a dismaying gift for imitating the worst features of Sarsaparilla. Naturally enough his enterprise is as unsuccessful as it is pitiable. White well shows, beneath this frenetic surface, the continued existence of Rosetree's true identity: as when the simultaneous approach of Passover and Easter (pp. 419-24) involves Rosetree in tension and confusion, expressed in irritability towards his office-girls, Miss Whibley and Miss Mudge. As one follows the dialogue on a certain afternoon, one is aware of a mounting impression that, whatever the reason, his irritability is giving place to a rough joviality and then a calm and amused ability to accept, for once, his real self. Thus Miss Whibley's insinuating remark that "her friend" is a quarter Jewish meets the reply:

A quarter Jew? So! A quarter Jew! I am a quarter shoe-fetichist, Miss Whibley, if that is what you wish to know. And five-eighths manic-depressive. That leaves still some small fraction to be accounted for. So we cannot yet work it out what I am. (p. 421)

After the others go home he works on, thinking of the mountain guest-house where his family is to spend Easter: " 'Along with a lot of bloody reffos,' Harry said." At last his strange mood is seen to stem from a faint but pervasive smell of cinnamon—something used by Miss Mudge for her chest—which has unconsciously borne him "down the passages of memory, right to the innermost chamber" where, in boyhood, he had taken part in the Passover. "Haïm Rosenbaum, the boy, had never cared for the stuff, but long after he had become a man . . . the scent of cinnamon remained connected with the deep joy of *Pessach*." When Himmelfarb comes in, his customary cold and Australianized reception from Rosetree becomes *"Shalom! Shalom! Mordecai!"* Although White is more explicit than he would need to be for a Jewish audience, the cinnamon is no arbitrary symbol imposed on unreceptive dialogue. By the time it is made explicit, one has been fully prepared by the dialogue itself.

Unfortunately for him—and for Himmelfarb—Rosetree does

not hold to this attitude through the episodes that follow. Foreseeing what will happen but torn by his more usual confusion of values (a confusion now represented also by a kaleidoscopic shifting in his mythic roles), he allows himself to be betrayed by events. After the crucifixion, however, he falls into a bitter and single-minded Judaic remorse. In this mood Rosetree—now Haïm ben Ya'akov—seeks out Mrs Godbold in order to give the body Jewish burial. In the scene that follows (pp. 498-503), Mrs Godbold offers him the news that Himmelfarb has been buried as a Christian on a morning "that clear" and "that still" that "we was glad to dawdle, and feel the sun lovely on our backs". She also offers him a consoling little sermon on the text that "except for the coat they are told to put on", all men are the same. And then, rising to an inspired pitch of solicitude, she offers him a cup of tea and some bread and quince-jam.

Setting aside, in a fervent if not confident incredulity, the Eucharistic possibilities of these objects, one is left to suppose that, as with the nice day they had for the funeral, we are in the presence of the Deep Human Simplicities. But Haïm ben Ya'akov is not to be consoled with bread and jam. What he needs is understanding, or even recognition, of the deep human complexity of his alienation. After denying his Judaism for the last time, he catches up her text and, muttering "It is the same! It is the same!", he goes away and kills himself.

Once or twice, perhaps, a flicker of irony is directed at the girlish impetuosity that lurks in Mrs Godbold's Junoesque frame. For a moment one's hopes are raised by the bread and jam, and by the failure of her consolations. But the narrator will no longer permit us to see Mrs Godbold as akin to Miss Docker: the only ironies that survive inspection are largely irrelevant to the real issues. Both her simplicities ("The loaves had risen golden. The scent was rushing out of them") and her loving-kindness ("all the time Mrs Godbold's stream flowed, warmer, stronger, all-healing") emerge unscathed. Presumably the suicide of Haïm ben Ya'akov is intended as an inevitable outcome of his role as Judas in the crucifixion-episode. In terms of the earlier part of the novel, however, he dies an unrecognized and poignantly unnecessary martyr to a monolithic and utterly insensitive loving-kindness that cannot accept men in their individuality but must insist on their absolute identity. And, in the same long-forgotten terms, it is this monstrous doctrine that Mrs Godbold survives to propagate.

Through a conversion of a Pauline suddenness and finality, the narrator has come to revere Mrs Godbold as a Magna Mater. It is not that her feet ever cease to be "planted firmly on the earth" (p. 552): the Magna Mater is never purely ethereal. Rather it is a matter of this ever-diminishing irony in the narrator's attitude and also of an ever-increasing recourse—culminating in the very last pages of the novel—to the traditional imagery of mystical exaltation. One's inability to share the joys of the narrator's conversion stems not only from what has already emerged but also from a quality of that mystical imagery to which we shall shortly return.

Even though the narrator has forgotten the earlier and better parts of the novel, we cannot, in a final judgment, afford to do so. Let us take the Chariot itself as a last instance of what has emerged from the proposition that, in a novel admittedly defective but far beyond the scope of simple formulae too categorically advanced, the mythic element is essentially related to contemporary issues as explored by White.

In the rich and subtle relationship that develops between Miss Hare and Himmelfarb, the Chariot is simply an epitome rather than a flimsy basis or an arbitrary link. Although each comes to know that the other is a "Charioteer" and although each gains from the relationship a renewed faith in his own Chariot, what they do for each other they do, first and foremost, as human beings. None of the other relationships among the *illuminati* is so fully explored, and the slightest of them (pp. 68-69) even impresses me as unintentionally comic. But both Dubbo and Himmelfarb are insecure enough to gain some comfort even from Mrs Godbold. And if Himmelfarb gains from Miss Hare an appreciation of the intuitive and the natural, he gains from Dubbo, in a moment of intense joy (pp. 348-51), the stimulus he needs to revive his stifled intellect and to enrich it, as never before, with what Miss Hare has taught him. Dubbo's profit from Himmelfarb, as we saw earlier, is also very great.

Nor does the Chariot solely, or even primarily, epitomize

the *interrelating* of the Riders. For each of them as an individual, his particular Chariot supplies a link with the past, whether as a personal memory or a rich communal tradition. (It thus helps, furthermore, to mark him off from the cultural rootlessness of Sarsaparilla.) And, especially but not only for Dubbo, the attaining of self-knowledge is manifested in an enrichment of his Chariot-vision.

At the same time, White's managing of the Chariot displays the most characteristic weakness of the novel, a weakness that manifests itself most obviously in a too frequent recourse to one or another of the stereotypes referred to. For all its felicities, the novel displays at bottom an irresoluteness about the precise effect it is seeking and an inclination to turn away into lax and self-indulgent gestures.

When Dubbo sets out to paint "the madwoman of Xanadu", his tenuous relationship with her gains super-sensory reinforcement, expressed in the imagery of light that consistently denotes the presence of the Chariot: "he had entered that brindled soul subtly and suddenly as light" (p. 510). Whatever one's private opinion of such exercises in the para-normal, one can conceive of—and even, as in *The Turn of the Screw*, recall—literary works which, by enveloping improbable circumstances in their own aura of conviction, demand, with an irresistible determination, the suspension of our disbeliefs. Unfortunately *Riders in the Chariot* is no such work.

The one condition, both necessary and sufficient, that governs the suspension of disbelief is that the work itself point both clearly and resolutely to the particular disbeliefs that need to be suspended. In *Riders in the Chariot* there are too many questions of importance on which the novel never makes up its mind. What, after all, is the "light" that enables Dubbo to enter "that brindled soul"? Is it simply a metaphor for imaginative insight? Is it the light traditionally associated with mystical exaltation? Or is it, alas, the light of that timorous and indecisive retreat into naturalism that can darken our understanding even of Himmelfarb:

The face of the Jew Himmelfarb immediately appeared to brim with light. The windows, of course, were blazing with it at that hour. (p. 424) 1/1965

Self and Shadow: The Quest for Totality in *The Solid Mandala*

THELMA HERRING

In tracing the development of a major writer one perceives continuity as well as growth: each new work is organically related to its predecessors, yet this does not preclude the possibility of surprise. Patrick White's latest novel has the capacity to surprise, though it proclaims its lineage unmistakably. Presenting, with a compression equalled only in *The Aunt's Story*, two lives as simple and ordinary to outward view as those of the Parkers in *The Tree of Man*, *The Solid Mandala* uses them to explore further the theme of man's potential divinity already treated on an epic scale in *Voss* and *Riders in the Chariot*: but to those (I confess I was among them) who wondered what path White could take after the latter novel *The Solid Mandala* provides a most impressive answer. He is still concerned with the necessity for love and humility in human relationships, with the inadequacy of reason and the superiority of the mystic's intuition of reality, but the division into the elect and the damned no longer seems so drastic as in *Riders in the Chariot*, and the efficacy of a life lived in love and humility is more attractively and persuasively exemplified. Less grand and ambitious in its design, the new novel is enriched by a deeper warmth of understanding, a broader humanity. Magnificent though parts of it are, *Riders in the Chariot*, like *The Tree of Man*, seems to me to suffer from a kind of externality: what most impresses is the artist's skill as a "maker", in the organization of his material and the sustaining of his design, whereas *The Solid Mandala* shares with *The Aunt's Story* and *Voss* a quality of inwardness, of the artist's immersion in the experiences he describes, which, for those readers who respond at all, engages the sympathies at a much deeper level—though of course the maker's skill is essential to their success. I see this trinity of novels as constituting White's greatest achievement so far.

The Solid Mandala is divided into four unequal parts. The brief opening and closing sections, in which the chief character is a Sarsaparillan housewife, Mrs Poulter, form a frame which puts the timeless theme in a contemporary context. In Part I Mrs Poulter is simply the dominant voice in a dialogue with "her small, dry, decent friend" Mrs Dun during a bus ride from Sarsaparilla to Barranugli, through which White gives preliminary information about the bachelor twin brothers, Waldo and Arthur Brown, living in retirement with their two dogs (appropriately named Scruffy and Runt), and exercises his mimetic skill in exposing the speech and mores of Australian suburbia. But what happens to the apparently commonplace Mrs Poulter in the course of the novel is one of its chief surprises and an essential part of its meaning.

The two central parts record events in the lives of Waldo and Arthur, told in the long second part from Waldo's point of view, then more briefly in the third from Arthur's. Although they are twins, and although "the lives of the brothers fused by consent at some points" (p. 82), they are opposites, physically, mentally and spiritually. Waldo the pseudo-intellectual, who excels at writing English essays, becomes a librarian and supposes himself to be superior, hates people, though he has aspirations as a novelist when he can find something to write about (he does manage to read a paper on Barron Field to the Beecroft Literary Society, and in old age finds a fragment of Tennyson's "Fatima" that he has copied out, and supposes it to be his own); Arthur the alleged simpleton, who is a failure at school except for a surprising flair for figures, becomes a grocer's assistant and humbly accepts inferior status but loves and is loved by people (and dogs). Their experiences, however, often coincide: they love the same woman (after their different fashions), both write "poems" and read books, each acquires a dog, both on occasion play the woman, both give Mrs Poulter a "child" (Waldo in the form of a plastic doll, Arthur by accepting the relationship himself), each is accosted by a whore on the night that the Second World War ends, each becomes in a sense the other's murderer. To Mrs Dun, watching from the bus as they walk hand in hand, "It was difficult to decide which was leading and which was led" (p. 19). Waldo, of course, believes himself to be the leader, and the protector of Arthur: whereas it emerges very clearly that Arthur, though he feels from the beginning that he is protected, is the protector of his whole family. Waldo and Arthur, in fact, are not ordinary twins, but rather a device for dramatizing the concept of the antithetical self, comparable with the opposition of Voss and Laura Trevelyan, and also recalling Dostoevsky's use of the Double or Doppelgänger type such as Raskolnikov and Ivan Karamazov, and Yeats's concept of the Mask. From the technical point of view the device is handled brilliantly: the twin narratives do not ask of the reader the kind of imaginative co-operation demanded by *Voss*, but Arthur's account is a check on Waldo's, showing how his apparent blunders are deliberate (as when he calls to the dogs *after* seeing Waldo in their mother's dress, to warn him of his presence).

Traversing most of the twins' life-span of seventy years, from the time when their parents bring them from England as small children, the story is from one point of view a chronicle of senescence and decay. Both parents die, the weatherboard house that George Brown has built for himself on arrival begins to disintegrate, the young quince-trees become wormy and woody, the sea of grass encroaches more and more, the young dogs, like the brothers themselves, grow old and feeble: in Waldo's part, startling images of squalor and decay (mice nesting in a burst leather chair, mutton fat curdling in skeins, and so on) enforce the impression of lives petering out in sterile loneliness (but also reflect the mental obliquity of Waldo). Some published accounts of the novel have, however, put a misleading emphasis upon this imagery: it is certainly striking, and important because the atmosphere it engenders prepares us for the horrifying climax, but it is by no means all-pervasive even in Waldo's part; in Arthur's part the prose is free of it but is rich in images with religious associations—the *decorum* of White's style in this novel deserves study. The scenes of old age in Part II are of a desolate and desolating sadness, but they are counterpointed, by means of time-shifts deftly manipulated through the associations of memory, against episodes from their earlier lives, which form the greater part of the narrative and contain some of the most brilliant comedy that White has given us. Within its relatively small compass the novel comprehends a remarkable range of moods and is beautifully proportioned.

Part II filters the story through the mind of an arch-egoist who has more in common with Joyce's mean, mediocre, life-denying Mr Duffy of the short story "A Painful Case" than with Meredith's superb Sir Willoughby Patterne: yet lucky the reader who does not feel at some point that Meredith's comment on Sir Willoughby, "He is all of us", applies to Waldo too. Though "hate" is the key word here, as "love" in the next section, it is not true to say that Waldo hates Arthur from the start: before his characteristic attitudes have hardened there are moments of affectionate communion that are touchingly rendered, but Waldo's life becomes a retreat into isolation, and though he can never escape from Arthur he increasingly resents this bondage. Compelled by Arthur to enter into their ritual union he remains "a plastic doll". The novelist systematically undermines all Waldo's pretensions, and his final judgment on him, conveyed through the dog's symbolic mutilation of his corpse, could not be harsher: yet the reader who remembers the all-too-human embarrassment of the young Waldo, writhing under the physical protection of his imbecile brother, the diffident warnings of his unworldly father, the patronage of the wealthy Mrs Musto, is likely to retain for him, even in his desiccated and self-cherishing old age, some grains of sympathy that may soften without fundamentally changing the verdict that White clearly invites us to make. The social agonies of a young outsider are incisively realized in the episode of Mrs Musto's tennis party, for instance:

Waldo hoped to withdraw, and did finally, to a less obvious position, behind a grazier of at least twenty, discussing rams with two young ladies worthy of his attention.
"But wool is so important," said one.
"Yes, I realize. But I'd be terrified," the other said, "of rams. I mean, they're sort of curlier, they're less direct than bulls."
Then all three exploded into fruit cup and understanding.
Waldo hated their aggressive white. He envied them the lan-

guage they spoke. Their eyes grew filmy observing over their shoulders somebody they had not known from childhood.

He went away. (pp. 88-9)

This quotation illustrates one facet of White's masterly management of tone. The style of the novel is austerer and more lucid than in his earlier books, and because so much of it reproduces the speech or thought of the characters there is frequent use of colloquial idiom (occasionally anachronistic, as when the schoolboy Waldo dismisses Arthur's talk as "dill's drivel"), but at other times it is the novelist's own cool, ironic voice that sounds through the prose, as in the passage quoted and such mocking comments as:

Not that he didn't despise Dulcie as well. In his crusade of bitterness there was only room for one ardent pauper. (p. 90)

and

Nobody remembered her husband, or knew whether she had ordered him out of existence so that she might enjoy a breezy widowhood. (p. 86)

More often White lends Waldo his own wit to express caustically judgments that are clearly Waldo's and characterize him more exactly in his vindictive malice than the person mentioned, as on the Dulcie of the future:

He did look back just once at Mrs Saporta, increasing, bulging, the Goddess of a Thousand Breasts, standing at the top of her steps, in a cluster of unborn, ovoid children. This giant incubator hoped she was her own infallible investment. But she would not suck him in. Imagining to hatch him out. (p. 158)

In the Feinstein scenes White produces superb social comedy from the encounter of the callow twins with the more sophisticated way of life of their Jewish friends; it would be hard to surpass anywhere in his work the passage in which Waldo reflects on the ways in which he would benefit by marriage with Dulcie:

... Then, the home. Undoubtedly he would benefit by having a home of his own. A bed to himself. And the meals Dulcie would prepare, rather dainty, foreign-tasting dishes, more digestible, more imaginative and spontaneously conceived. Because food to Mother was something you couldn't avoid, and which she had always offered with a sigh. But it was his work, his real work, which would benefit most. The atmosphere in which to evolve a style. The novel of psychological relationships in a family, based on his own experience, for truth, illuminated by what his imagination would infuse. One of the first things he intended to do was buy a filing cabinet to instal in his study. (p. 150)

Matching the warmth that is communicated in the scenes of the civilized, closely knit family life of the Feinsteins is the muted sympathy that tempers the gently ironic presentation of the twins' parents. George Brown, the shy, bookish bank clerk, and his socially superior wife, proud of her Quantrell heritage (with which Waldo in turn is obsessed), are in some ways reminiscent of George and Julia Goodman in *The Aunt's Story*: but the characterization of the snobbish mother is notably more tolerant, and Anne Brown is redeemed not only by her genuine love for her renegade Baptist but also by her ability to criticize the conventions of the world she has renounced. Thus, although Waldo is very much his mother's son, he stands alone in his incapacity to love, his retreat from any genuine involvement in life, and he alone is denied the author's compassion.

In the end Waldo dies of his hatred, willing Arthur's death: but the most finely imagined expression of that hatred is the scene in the Public Library in which he denies his shabby, simple brother as well as physically ejecting him. The betrayal is shocking, yet so dramatically is the scene rendered that one feels the unbearable pressure on Waldo, tempting him to reject, even while understanding as he does not the cost to his humanity of that rejection. The searing pain that it inflicts is felt for Waldo as much as for Arthur, not least in the sequel, which the simplicity of the writing makes profoundly poignant:

In the evening he returned as usual to Sarsaparilla, carrying a small parcel of New Zealand cod he had bought for their tea . . . He was so tired he would not have been able to resist the figure in the old raincoat, for he realized the other side of Lidcombe that his brother was sitting ahead of him. Arthur either remained unaware, or made no attempt to approach, anyway, there and then.

For at Barranugli he came and sat, equably, silently, beside Waldo in the Sarsaparilla bus, and they remained together after getting down.

As they walked down Terminus Road, Waldo realized that, somewhere, he had left his parcel of New Zealand cod. He was too tired to care. (p. 202)

Part II, then, is a merciless exposure of the mind of Waldo Brown: but towards the end Arthur's reading of *The Brothers Karamazov* and his writing of a poem prepare for the religious orientation of Part III. Very early the crucial question rises in the half-sleeping consciousness of the child Arthur, after he has been taken to a performance of *Götterdämmerung*: "Who and where were the gods?" (p. 217), and it is remarkable how many varieties of religion, Eastern and Western, ancient and modern, are referred to, either directly or implicitly, in the course of the novel. Brought up by parents who are conscientious unbelievers, Arthur is untroubled by religious questions until in old age he becomes perplexed by the problem of pain and the Christian emphasis on "the blood and the nails", and begins the search for his identity, which he finds, however, "not through words, but by lightning". To Dulcie Feinstein, with whom he experiences spiritual union, he is the instrument through whom her dying father is reunited to God; and to Mrs Poulter in the last section, entitled "Mrs Poulter and the Zeitgeist", he becomes the object of faith when her God is brought crashing down by the shock of the discovery of Waldo's defiled body:

"This man would be my saint," she said, "if we could still believe in saints. Nowadays," she said, "we've only men to believe in. I believe in this man." (p. 315)

The roles of these two women, Dulcie and Mrs Poulter, may be compared with those of Mrs Godbold and Miss Hare in *Riders in the Chariot*. Both are on the symbolic level earth goddesses, Dulcie through her fecundity, Mrs Poulter through her closeness to nature:

She had a little black pig which ran rootling round the back yard. She could lift the combs out of the hives without ever bothering to put on a veil. She stored pears on high shelves, the burn fading out of her skin towards the armpits. (p. 260)

It is perhaps with reference to the metaphorical sense of dark as "chthonic" that they both have dark hair. The symbolic use of physical characteristics is in fact a marked feature of the novel. Arthur's brown eyes link him not only with his gentle father but also with Dulcie, Len Saporta, and their children (nor is it perhaps irrelevant to note that Dulcie has "the eyes of certain dogs"—Arthur's comprehensive love embraces dogs equally with humans), while Waldo with his "inherited eyes", pale and cold, is linked with the mother whose aristocratic connections fascinate him, and feels an affinity with other blue-eyed people.

The main device for linking characters is, however, the central symbol of the novel, Arthur's four marbles or "solid mandalas" which signify the integrity of the self. (The Sanskrit word "mandala", denoting the ritual or magic circle used in Lamaism and in Tantric yoga as an aid to contemplation, is used to signify the self or totality.) Dulcie and Mrs Poulter are each given one of the marbles; the flawed or knotted marble, intended for Waldo, is rejected by him and finally lost; Arthur keeps the whorled one for himself. But the mandala symbolism extends much further. Jung points out in his discussion of this subject that lamaistic mandalas are based on a quaternary system (hence the number of Arthur's marbles and the four corners of his mandala dance) and that the figure of the square often gives the idea of a house or temple—which surely explains the insistence on the shape of the Browns' house with its Greek pediment. (Retrospectively, one can see that the chariot with its four riders was also a mandala symbol.) In fact, by imagery and allusion White constructs a network of mandala symbols: the wheel, the lotus, the rose (it is perhaps significant that Arthur refers to a wreath of roses framing Waldo when he puts on his mother's blue dress, since this cryptically described incident seems to suggest a vain search for totality through his family heritage), the Star of David which Len Saporta gives to Dulcie, the central design in Saporta's carpet, the rock crystal, the sun (and I have an uneasy suspicion that the orange ju-jubes which orange-haired Arthur asks for when he is led away, like Theodora in *The Aunt's Story*, to an asylum are solar surrogates).

There are, too, allusions to a series of androgynous figures also symbolic of wholeness: Tiresias, Christ (often represented as an androgyne) and "hermaphroditic Adam", who "carries about with him Eve, or his wife, hidden in his body", which suggests to the bisexual Arthur a similar mystical relationship between himself and both Dulcie and Mrs Poulter. (The passage which Arthur reads in "some book" is quoted in Jung's *Psychology and Alchemy*, and it may well be that Arthur's dream of a tree growing out of his thighs with Dulcie's face among the leaves and of Mrs Poulter's skin turning into bark was suggested by an alchemical picture of Adam with a tree growing out of him reproduced in the same book.)

Through this submerged symbolism drawn from the great religions and mythologies of the world White reinforces with a poet's synthesizing power the religious implications of his theme: the exquisite image of the Chinese woman under the wheel-tree, for instance, is associated with Arthur's dancing of the mandala, described in brilliantly evocative prose which gathers up many of the symbolic images: the dying gods, the moon, the orange sun, the Star, the pears and pigs and golden honey, the blood of the Passion. (In its expression of the four lives the dance may be compared with Dubbo's painting of the four riders in the Chariot.) The varied symbolism points to the truth not of any one creed, but of that "perennial philosophy" which mystics of all faiths share, but in its Eastern rather than its Western form, acknowledging no difference between the human and the divine essence—expressed for instance in Hinduism in the belief that "the indwelling Atman [Self] is the same as Brahman [the Absolute]".[1] Though Arthur acknowledges no gods, he can apprehend ultimate reality— "offering his prayer to what he knew from light or silences" (p. 265)—and in the end, divinity is seen to be immanent in him.

Any difficulty one may experience in perceiving White's meaning is inherent in his theme: he has never been at such pains to give his readers clues, not only through the titles of books that Arthur reads but also through the definition of "mandala" that he finds in an encyclopaedia. I would myself be inclined to regret the rather too obviously contrived intro-

---

[1] Aldous Huxley, introduction to *Bhagavad-Gita*, translated by Swami Prabhavananda and Christopher Isherwood.

duction of this last clue, but at any rate only readers who add to a forgivable ignorance an unforgivable laziness (under which head I subsume "words on the page" fanatics) could conceivably complain.

That Arthur should accuse *himself* of failing in love explains his readiness to accept responsibility for Waldo's death: "he saw the hatred Waldo was directing, had always directed, at all living things" but blames himself as "the getter of pain". In this way Arthur, who could not understand "this Christ stuff", recognizes "their common pain". A reference to "their lives, or life" (p. 295) stresses the nature of their relationship. At this climax he finds his identity, achieves true totality and so is himself a mandala, "the dwelling of the god".

Thus Arthur is conceived as a person whose outward deficiencies humanize without undermining his inner perfection. It is a daring conception, even for a writer who specializes in saintly eccentrics, but as character rather than symbol Arthur, compared with Waldo, who is so thoroughly known, is less than totally coherent: I cannot quite reconcile the reading Arthur with the Arthur whom everyone regards as a "dill". Yet even Dostoevsky was very conscious of the problem of presenting "a positively good man" when writing *The Idiot*: the difficulties are enormous and White has done well in producing some memorable moments of tenderness in Arthur's silent communion with friends.

About what he achieves through Mrs Poulter I have no reservations at all. In her childlessness the counterpart of Miss Hare, in her innocent sexuality and simple piety (of a much more casual kind however) she is akin to Mrs Godbold, but is a far more sympathetic, though (or because) spiritually more imperfect, character than that monolithic hound of heaven (one cannot imagine Mrs Poulter pursuing her beloved though neglectful husband into a brothel). That Mrs Poulter, through the simple humanity that enables her to find answers to Arthur's questions and to respond to his goodness with affection, can earn a mandala and burn with Arthur "in a fit of understanding or charity" (p. 310) seems to imply that a measure of illumination is attainable by most people. When Arthur recalls the afternoon of the mandala dance he remembers "skin smelling ever so faintly of struck flint" (p. 288): it may be fanciful to associate this image with the title of Henry Vaughan's *Silex Scintillans* and the emblem of the flashing flint, but at any rate it seems that Mrs Poulter is granted a moment of mystical apprehension through Arthur's dance, so that at the end it is she who bears witness to his apotheosis before "re-entering her actual sphere of life", and sees their two faces becoming one at the centre of Arthur's whorled marble.

Uncompromising in its condemnation of dedicated egoism, *The Solid Mandala* is nevertheless one of White's most humane as well as most integrated novels. To read it is a scarifying experience—but it scarifies to heal. In itself remarkable evidence of his powers as a novelist, it seems also to hint that even now those powers have not developed their utmost reach.

3/1966

II SOME RECONSIDERATIONS

"Jardin Exotique": The Central Phase of *The Aunt's Story*

J. F. BURROWS

Theodora Goodman is nearly fifty when she leaves Australia. Twenty years have passed since the death of her father, whom she had still loved fondly even after his ineffectuality had cost him her respect, and since the loss of Meroë, her first and only home. She has spent those twenty years as companion to a mother whose lifelong hatred of her she has almost learnt to match; as devoted aunt to Lou Parrott, the unloved daughter of her sister Fanny and of a discarded suitor of her own; and as a lonely spinster whose quiet integrity is dearer to her than the material comforts of a marriage of convenience.

Now, upon the death of her mother, she tries to celebrate her freedom without quite knowing what she means by the word. Her immediate sense of release is qualified more sharply than she realizes by the nervous gestures of her hands, the trembling of her mouth, her need to reassure herself "many times"[1] that she really is free, and her faintly-surprised discovery of a certain grief. Her independence of those still living is less absolute than she supposes when—afraid that "there is no life-line to other lives" (p. 137) and that it is not for her "to dispose of life and death, as if they were presents wrapped in tissue paper" (p. 17)—she feels that she cannot attempt to assuage Lou's fear of death. Besides being shown that her actual freedom is more limited than she supposes, we are enabled to share her own sense that even Ithaca[2] has lost its mean-

---

[1] *The Aunt's Story* (Second edition, 1958), p. 10. All page references are to this edition.
[2] The novel's Homeric references are discussed by Thelma Herring, "Odyssey of a Spinster: A Study of *The Aunt's Story*", *Southerly*, pp. 12-16 above.

85

ing for her. A visionary Ithaca had sustained her father against the onslaughts of his wife, and the young Theodora had come to share his vision. But the long years have dulled its force. When she does set sail, it is because she can afford a gesture in the direction of half-forgotten pieties.

Most critics of *The Aunt's Story* have been content to celebrate the "actuality" of Part One and to circumvent the difficulties that begin, less than halfway through the novel, when Theodora leaves Australia. The belief that Part Two is a verbal chaos, a long-drawn out evocation of Theodora's madness, has been taken as a warrant for its neglect.

Yet those who hold to this belief are in bad company. In the novel itself, Theodora is called mad only by such monsters of normality as Mrs Goodman, Fanny, and the ignorant strangers of Part Three, all of them glad to evade the problems posed by Theodora's disturbing behaviour. It is not that Theodora is "normal" but that White persistently undermines conventional antitheses between normality and madness, as between good and evil and between actuality and dream. The words of Sokolnikov, wisest of the novel's impostors, always repay attention. When he, in turn, is charged with madness, he replies, " 'Whenever the answer is not in bronze, that is the cry of the middle classes' " (p. 190).

I hope to show that, so far from being a verbal chaos, Part Two stands in its own right and as a natural issue from Part One: for Theodora's European experience consists very largely in facing problems of her earlier life. But, even if this hypothesis falls down, there is less change in her than the customary account suggests: *sidere mens eadem mutato*. The most obvious example lies in the familiar images that new occasions still evoke: the roses and the warm, yellow stone of Meroë itself, the Abyssinian associations of its name, and the dormant fires of its black, volcanic hills; the greenish light, filtering through the pine-trees into her father's study, and the bearded figure at the desk; the garnet rings of her mother's disciplined hands; the pink, artificial flowers of Fanny's facile charms; and her own struggles to find a personal "music".

Theodora's essential habits of mind change little more than her memories. Her desire for truth is always accompanied by the honesty and humility to accept it when it offers. Her austerity in judging herself is always accompanied by a compassionate reluctance to judge others. And, above all, she shows from childhood a remarkable gift of empathy, an ability to see through the eyes of other creatures, to enter their very minds, and to discover in them new aspects of herself. She is shooting rabbits one day at Meroë when she comes upon just such a creature:

> The little hawk tore and paused, tore and paused. Soon he would tear through the wool and the maggots and reach the offal in the belly of the sheep. Theodora looked at the hawk. She could not judge his act, because her eye had contracted, it was reddish-gold, and her curved face cut the wind. Death, said Father, lasts for a long time. Like the bones of the sheep that would lie, and dry, and whiten, and clatter under horses. But the act of the hawk, which she watched, hawk-like, was a moment of shrill beauty that rose above the endlessness of bones. The red eye spoke of worlds that were brief and fierce. (p. 33)

Unlike many a half-baked nature mystic, fictional or real, Theodora is not prevented by her gift of empathy from seeing that there is much in human life too complex to be analogous to the starkly instinctive life of a hawk. Once or twice, admittedly, she allows herself to over-simplify. On a later expedition, this time with Frank Parrott—then young, single, and "functional within his limits" (p. 14)—she is torn between sexual desire and a growing awareness of his brutishness. Seeing the hawk once more, she longs for a hawk-like flight into beauty and freedom. Ignoring her pleas, Frank shoots—and misses. In a turmoil of emotions, she clutches at another way to freedom, a symbolic suicide, a destruction of the life she might have led with him, a use of the hawk as instinctive as its own use of the sheep:

> Theodora had begun to laugh. She knew with some fear and pleasure that she had lost control. This, she said, is the red eye. And her vision tore at the air, as if it were old wool on a dead sheep. She was as sure as the bones of a hawk in flight.
> Now she took her gun. She took aim, and it was like aiming at her own red eye. She could feel the blood-beat the other side of the membrane. And she fired. And it fell. It was an old broken umbrella tumbling off a shoulder. (p. 73)

As Theodora quickly sees, this is no solution at all. Her own conflict about Frank, briefly assuaged, flares up again at the ball that shortly follows. Frank is aware of nothing more than a blow to his vanity. And the hawk is dead.

Such simplicistic moments grow rare as Theodora matures. Indeed the most striking instance in all Part One is less remarkable for her being tempted by a drastically simple solution than for her recognizing, in sufficient time, that it is no more a solution than the shooting of the hawk had been. Towards the end of her life, Mrs Goodman succeeds at last in driving Theodora beyond endurance. As she prepares to kill her mother, however, Theodora regains her self-command. She recognizes that, like the hawk, her mother is what she is and acts only in accordance with her nature. She recognizes that, for her own part, the murder would afford her a release from servitude but would cost her all the memories that she cherishes. Her real problem, yet far from solution, is somehow to come to terms with her mother; and, to this problem, the projected murder is only incidental:

But this, she trembled, does not cut the knot. She threw back the thin knife, which fell and clattered on the zinc . . . It has been close, felt Theodora . . . (p. 128)

Even at such a moment, her honesty reminds her that she is not a hawk: "I am guilty of a murder that has not been done, she said, it is the same thing, blood is only an accompaniment."

In the wool, the maggots, and the tearing beak, in the old broken umbrella tumbling off a shoulder, and in the thin knife clattering on the zinc, there are signs of the actuality White's critics have praised. Beneath and beyond it, however, lies a richer actuality, the shape of a complex personality modified but not shattered by a harsh experience of life. Such are the difficulties of Part Two that the remaining discussion must be directed to them. In leaving Part One and the brief Part Three to speak for themselves, I am persuaded that they speak more plainly than Part Two. And, if my account of Part Two is meaningful, it will imply an account of what leads up to it and follows from it.

Part Two begins upon Theodora's arrival, after perhaps five years of unchronicled travel, at a dreary little hotel on the

French Riviera. Persuaded that she has lost touch with her fellow-humans, she has come there for a revived communion with "tree and flower" (p. 142) in the *jardin exotique* which is the boast of the establishment. Even granting the austerity of her tastes, the garden is not quite what she had bargained for. The very hotel comes vividly to life beside this:

> static, rigid . . . equation of a garden . . . *Notre jardin exotique*, Monsieur Durand has said, but his pronoun possessed only diffidently. . . . This was a world in which there was no question of possession. In its own right it possessed, and rejected, absorbing just so much dew with its pink and yellow mouths, coldly tearing at cloth or drawing blood. The garden was untouchable. (p. 146)

Overcome by the hostility of the garden, Theodora comes quickly to feel that even "though she had not yet seen them, . . . the hotel was full of people, and she waited to touch their hands" (p. 147). The people being what they are, this is to be a curious process; and one cannot wonder at Theodora's needing for some time to clutch at familiar objects, especially her own few worldly goods. *Les demoiselles* Bloch are honest mice, picking for ever at the crumbs of the past. Wetherby, a poet-cum-remittance man, and the decadent Lieselotte, deserted by a husband who is perhaps a German count, live at each other's mercy in what passes here as love. Mrs Rapallo, an American *émigrée*, exists in the vicarious blaze of her daughter's glory as *Principessa dell' Isola Grande*. Sokolnikov, an exiled Russian general, seems only a ludicrous grotesque. And even the young and pretty Katina Pavlou has been deserted by her parents and, accompanied by a stodgy English maid-companion, passes from hotel to dreary hotel. Katina Pavlou excepted, each one's dominant concern in life is the preservation of his own imposture. Towards his fellows, each of them displays only apathy or veiled hostility. For all this, Theodora's association with them is to prove more rewarding than first appearances would suggest; and her belief that she has lost touch with mankind is to prove no more than the disorientation of a traveller newly-arrived. As it develops, her association with them is to fall into two phases: that where, in Sokolnikov's words, Theodora "creates the illusion of other people"; and that where, "once created, they choose their own realities" (p. 250).

In the eighty pages of the first phase, there is little external action. Theodora meets her fellow guests, walks with one, visits the room of another, or talks with a third in the *jardin* (which she gradually finds more tolerable). The real emphasis of this part of the novel is on what may be called Theodora's fugue-life. In speaking of "fugues", I would admit the word's connotations of flight, but would regard them as secondary to the creation of "a painful, personal music, of which the themes were intertwined" (p. 174). To the extent that Theodora's fugues are flights, it is as imaginative projections of herself into these other lives, and not as retreats from "reality". What she is doing is facing her own problems in the subtly altered perspectives that these other lives afford. This fugal period must—and does—end when Theodora's increasing knowledge of the "actual" Katina Pavlou, the "actual" Sokolnikov, necessitates an admission, so to speak, of their right to an independent existence.

White's first exercise in a narrative mode for which there are many rough but perhaps no exact analogues makes plain what he is about and asks no more of us than do those passages of Part One where, for example, Theodora identifies herself with the hawk. Very soon after arriving at the hotel, Theodora is sitting in the *jardin* when Katina Pavlou runs in, followed by Grigg, the maid-companion. They begin to talk to each other but not to Theodora, whom they have never seen. Before a dozen sentences have passed, "Theodora Goodman had become a mirror, held to the girl's experience. Their eyes were interchangeable, like two distant, unrelated lives mingling for a moment in sleep" (p. 148). A moment later the girl says to Grigg,

"There was an earthquake, do you remember? And we ran and lay on the beach. There was a black island that shook."
Theodora trembled for the black island. She looked across at the opposite shore . . .
"Miss Theodora," said Katina, or her small extinct voice, "I think that the wind has died."
"Yes," said Theodora, "it is most surely dead." (p. 149)

Theodora, evidently, has assumed the role of governess to Katina, a role which, wholly in her imagination, she enacts for more than two pages. It ends with her return to a "reality" in which Katina is still voicing the remark that had evoked this whole fugue:

> Theodora held the body of the child. She felt the moment of death and life. Across the water a black island moved, quite distinctly, under a chalky puff of cloud.
> "There was an earthquake," the girl said. "Do you remember?"
> In the *jardin exotique* a wind was creaking through the fingers of the cactus. (p. 151)

After this first, straightforward indication of what he is about, White takes it increasingly for granted and moves from "reality" to fugue, fugue to "reality" with increasingly subtle, though always exact, signals to us.

White's purposes are more important to us than his signalling-devices; but let us avoid premature judgments and see what emerges from the fugues themselves. The meaning of this first one is simple in itself and has been clearly foreshadowed in Part One. Theodora's attention is first captured, of course, by her associating the "black island that shook" with the black volcanic hills of Meroë. In what follows, detail after detail takes up the concerns of the younger Theodora; but the central points lie in her assumption of the characteristically humble role of governess and in the confidence with which she assuages the girl's fear of death. In this latter aspect, her imagined behaviour stands in immediate contrast to Grigg's actual brusqueness and in less explicit contrast to her own earlier treatment of Lou Parrott, to which I have previously referred. Not that Theodora allows this vicarious second chance to absolve her of her original failure: austere as ever, she regards her fugue as a spurious comforter, an indulgence more contemptible than her mother's aspirin tablets.

By virtue of her friendliness and her increasingly evident resemblance to Lou Parrott, not all of it the work of Theodora's imagination, Katina Pavlou becomes too "easy" a subject to warrant a continued fugal approach. Apart from a brief and brilliantly ironical fugue in which Theodora, still as governess, draws analogies between Katina's parents and her own as selfish and discontented globe-trotters (p. 186; cf. pp. 25-26, 87), Theodora's later dealings with Katina Pavlou are usually more direct. (Of Katina's other role as Sokolnikov's "little Varvara" and the effect of that role on Theodora, it is too soon to speak.)

Theodora's associations with the other inhabitants of the Hôtel du Midi do not all develop into genuine relationships. Before considering those that do, let us touch briefly on the lesser associations, not only for what they severally reveal but also as a cumulative illustration of the flexibility of White's fugal mode.

In their unobtrusive but absolute concern with themselves and in the narrowness of the selves that concern them, the sisters Bloch have little to offer to anyone: what Theodora sees of them, therefore, never approaches a state of fugue.

Wetherby, on the other hand, poses something of a problem for Theodora. For a short time she is attracted to him, associates him as poet with Moraïtis, the 'cellist she had known in Sydney, and relieves her starved maternal impulses by envisaging herself as his mother (pp. 160, 170-71). Delighted to find a new audience, however, Wetherby turns almost at once to an obsessive and self-pitying account of his sufferings at the hands of a domineering patroness. Theodora does not yet see that the case of Muriel Leese-Leese presents, in a radically altered perspective, the case of Julia Goodman. (Thus Wetherby's insistence that Mrs Leese-Leese exerted a god-like power over her minions revives a charge that Theodora had once [p. 134] laid at her mother's door.) Quickly sensing, however, that he cannot participate in any true relationship, Theodora observes his life, as she envisages it, from the safely impersonal standpoint of a piece of furniture:

"Even [Wetherby tells her] in what one thought was the security of one's own room, with its ugly, haphazard furniture, one was never altogether safe from Muriel Leese-Leese."

Listening to the history of Wetherby, unfolding as logically as the shadow from the root of a cactus, *Theodora was not aware that it was meant for her*. Rather, she was some haphazard cupboard in his comparatively secure, ugly room, in which he proposed to arrange his thoughts. In the circumstances her shoulders grew angular with expectation. She composed her grain. (p. 172; my italics)

After this fugal essay, her experience of him is long confined to what she unwillingly overhears from the bedroom adjoining her own, where he and Lieselotte lacerate each other and themselves.

On meeting Lieselotte, Theodora's first response is to invest the ex-countess and her lost castle with a vague aura of past splendour. These fancies wither when she is told how the pseudo-medievalism of Lieselotte's Siegfried-figure had turned into "a myth in jackboots" (p. 174). Neither Theodora nor the reader ever really learns what truth there is in Lieselotte's account of herself. True or not, both the tale and the woman who tells it strike home in Theodora. For Lieselotte reincarnates Julia Goodman the wife in her intense but tight-reined sexuality, her marriage to a man whose life was real only when it was mythic, and her lust—cause or consequence?—for destruction (pp. 174-76). These analogies become evident to the reader even before Theodora gives up her romance of the medieval countess. But Theodora's growing knowledge of Lieselotte gradually brings her to see the Goodmans' married life in a new light. At the end of an overheard quarrel between Lieselotte and Wetherby, Theodora rises to an unprecedented admission: " . . . it is no longer possible, sighed Theodora Goodman, to distinguish which is which" (p. 208).

The globe-trotting socialite, the domineering mother, the frustrated wife: it begins to seem that, for all her travels, Theodora is never far from home and mother. Yet, neurotic though she may be, this is not the endless, futile retrogression of insanity but a determined and at last successful confrontation of old problems in new contexts. Thanks to the anguished searchings of Part Two (" . . . apart, armed, twisted, dreamless, admitting at most the echoes of sound, the gothic world": p. 152), Mrs Goodman is no longer a force in Part Three, where the only person who resembles her is observed by Theodora in a spirit of quiet amusement and wry compassion, with even a trace of admiration.

Then, again, the novel advances on a broader front than paraphrase suggests. Certainly the life of minor figures like Wetherby and Lieselotte does not range far beyond Theodora's conception of them. Yet, through the fluidity of White's rendering, even they display a measure of vitality. In the Blochs, it is manifest in their uneasy attempts at idiomatic English, their catching up of each other's phrases, and their melancholy timidity. In Wetherby, it is a function of his utter absorption in his dreary little selfhood. And even Lieselotte's monomaniacal hostility varies from downright savagery and exquisite sadism to an almost amused contempt. Even tiny extracts, put side by side, show signs of this vitality and of White's skill in differentiating it:

"We have been walking," explained Mademoiselle Marthe . . . "On the coast road there is a small round tower which has some connexion with Napoleon, though we forget what."

"It is agreeable to sit there, in the scenery," said Mademoiselle Berthe, "and talk about things that happened while the world was still comparatively safe to live in." . . .

"They say, you know, that Hitler will make a war."

"Or the Communists will take over."

"Or perhaps we shall be subjected to both events." (p. 153)

"I suppose I should introduce myself," said the young man. "My name is quite ordinary. It is Wetherby. I am from Birmingham, where my mother still lives in a brick house. My father, needless to say, was a clergyman. He was a shy, dry man, to whom I never found anything to say . . . But my mother, she is a different matter. She invariably wears blue. At the minor public school to which I was sent, I used to apologise for her protruding teeth." (pp. 170-71)

"Oh, he!" said Lieselotte. "Yes. By nature he is the hero of an operetta. But he chose to be a disinfectant. To disinfect the world." (p. 174)

Partly through a richer comic vitality, partly through the mutual antagonism that so often sparks it off, but also through their coming to mean more to Theodora, Mrs Rapallo and Sokolnikov achieve another dimension.

In common with Lieselotte, Mrs Rapallo first enters the novel as a living embodiment of the European past. Ignoring the better-informed but violently-conflicting opinions of the other guests, Theodora is "enchanted by the gouty golden music", "stiff and brocaded, formal as some flutes" (p. 161).

This performance is not without its cost: "She was put together painfully, rashly, ritually, crimson over purple. Her eyes glittered, but her breath was grey" (p. 162).

Setting aside the evidence of her own eyes and undismayed to learn that an American heart beats in this brocaded breast, Theodora shortly afterwards embarks on the least substantial of all her fugues. For us, though not consciously for her, it is a mockingly over-stressed parody of those quasi-Jamesian novelettes into which Edith Wharton degenerated and beyond which Scott Fitzgerald too seldom rose. Theodora sees herself as companion—the humble role again—to the young Elsie van Tuyl in a mansion where everything but the dark, mysterious Rapallo was "sure, substantial, silver", where "the buttons strained and kept the upholstery down", where

> At night when the older women, who had played their cards, sat amongst the whatnots in their diamonds talking of Europe, and the older men, quite grey and gnarled from minting money, minted it still, in their conversation of steel and steam and supernumerary souls, music melted the gardenia trees for the glorious young, who were still hesitating to sell themselves. (pp. 165-66)

If oppressed by these splendours, one can always take refuge in " 'the shack. Just the two of us. Alone. We shall walk in the lanes, and gather blueberries, and feel the rain on us, and watch the emerald beetles' " (p. 166). Knowing her novelettes too well to have Elsie marry her eligible young man, Theodora has her elope to Europe with Rapallo in the untroubled consciousness that " 'I am rich. I can buy my way out' " (p. 167).

Two more Rapallo-fugues are to follow when Theodora's acquaintance with the woman has progressed a little. The first (pp. 194-95) is less a creation of Theodora's own than a visualizing, through Theodora's eyes, of Mrs Rapallo's glorification of her daughter's wealth and influence as *Principessa dell' Isola Grande*. The second (pp. 198-99), much more Theodora's creation, is a menopausal daydream about the still mysterious Mr Rapallo, wealthy and virile, bearing traces of the men she might herself have married—and yet a person of no consequence in the lives of his wife and daughter.

All three of these fugues tend in the same directions. In all of them Theodora plays a more than usually passive role and, in all of them, the figures she sees are shadowy and unreal. Now there is no question of a lapse in White's control here: his parody is never more brilliant, and it is Theodora herself who is ironically placed before us. After all, she need only have listened to the woman to know that, whatever her secrets, they could not be those of a novelette of high life:

"Gloria had a vocation for the world," Mrs Rapallo explained. "I mean, even as a kid Gloria was *distinguée*. She had poise. You would have been surprised, Miss Goodman, at her grasp of current affairs. Her touch on the pianoforte was quite lovely. At fifteen she had a smattering of several languages. She had even begun to master Rumanian, with the help of a gentleman we met in Cairo. And most important, she could wear clothes. So it was only to be expected that Nino—that is my son-in-law, the Principe —should be impressed. Naturally it also cost a little." (pp. 193-94)

At bottom we are being shown Theodora's ignorance and puzzlement in the face of the essentially unreal, a matter to which we shall return. These fugues also give rise to a more immediate point.

In all of them, Theodora is romanticizing the ostentatious display of wealth when it is carried to an extreme pitch. So blinded, she overlooks for a time the resemblances between Mrs Rapallo and Gloria on the one hand and Mrs Goodman and Fanny on the other. And, in overlooking them, she is for the time accepting the vulgar fantasies of wealth for which Fanny especially had been distinguished (pp. 30, 97) and forsaking the attitude that she and her father had always taken to material possessions: "Our Place is a decent size, not so big as Parrotts' or Trevelyans', but my Father says big enough for peace of mind" (p. 23). While Theodora's reaction against what she has always felt is too extreme to endure, it is well for her to be shaken out of her complacency. No doubt it is more admirable to accept inherited wealth with urbanity than to flaunt it in the face of society. Yet the vulgarity of Mrs Elton is only a few generations less practised than the complacency that prevails at Mansfield Park. And, for all her vulgarity, the ostentation of a Mrs Rapallo can spring from a real need. The whole question is one that Theodora will be obliged to ponder more seriously than she would ever have supposed. It comes to a head in the clash between Mrs Rapallo and Sokolnikov over the nautilus-shell, a clash we must now approach from Sokolnikov's side.

The essential vitality of Sokolnikov, the peak of the novel's comic achievement, lies in his unique blending of worldly disillusionment with a continuing dependence upon the illusory, of a mostly tolerant scepticism with an irrepressible joy in life. When Katina Pavlou tells him, "hopelessly, with all the conviction of her age, 'life is full of sadness' " (p. 182), his answer epitomizes his whole career: " ' . . . you must let me teach you that abstractions are a great mistake. If I do not always follow my own precept, it is because the concrete often offers itself in a somewhat unattractive form' " (p. 183).

In three episodes that constitute the longest and most important of all her fugues, Theodora learns of Sokolnikov's history and places her own interpretation on it. She is to find, however, that his version is very different and that, just as he and the others are actors in her fugues, so she and Katina Pavlou have parts to play in his. The "facts" of it all are simple enough. As a middle-aged bachelor, Alyosha Sergei Sokolnikov had lived with his spinster sister, Ludmilla, who was sallow, mannish, and austere. Opposed by her jealous good-sense and by the scorn of Anna Stepanovna, an elderly and aristocratic relative, Alyosha Sergei's last and rather ludicrous wooing of the young and beautiful Varvara had ended in her marrying another man. Later, during the 1917 Revolution, Anna Stepanovna had been executed. Fleeing for the border in disguise, he and Ludmilla had been captured by Bolsheviks who shot her while he, unable to save her, escaped into lifelong exile. As they re-live these events, he and Theodora concur in seeing her as Ludmilla and Katina Pavlou as Varvara. But whereas Theodora sees her own parents in him and Anna Stepanovna, he sees only himself and Anna.

The gradual evolution between Theodora and Alyosha Sergei of "that complementary curse and blessing, a relationship" (p. 210) occupies about a third of Part Two and is notable, even in *The Aunt's Story*, for the closeness of its texture. " 'Your branch of the family, Ludmilla, never knew what to do with its hands'" (p. 181), says Anna Stepanovna: and we are back in the drawing-room at Meroë, with Theodora painfully trying to play Chopin. Or Ludmilla jealously pictures how "Varvara swam against the waltz, and they stood in the open doorways, applauding, as she dashed the water from her swan breast" (p. 178): and we are back at the Parrotts' ball, where Theodora had "caught fire" but where Fanny, a swan on the sea of waltz-music (pp. 75, 77), had still been the popular success of the evening. Since Alyosha Sergei's version of a hundred such moments is continuously juxtaposed with Theodora's, there can be no question of our tracing the growth of their relationship in its details: a summary account of leading issues must suffice.

On Sokolnikov's side, Theodora is of little *active* help. Insisting that "'only women like Anna Stepanovna think they can regulate life'" (p. 179), he rejects Theodora's attempts to rescue him from Katina-Varvara. The eventual resolution of his relationship with Katina Pavlou is not Theodora's but their own.

And yet, by their mere existence, Theodora and Katina Pavlou aid him profoundly. Contrary to his own belief, he is not an egoistic cynic. For twenty years he has fought valiantly against becoming obsessed by sentimental daydreams of his "bright Varvara", his "singing bird" (p. 177), and against denying himself all memory of the sister he had left dying. Merely by existing, Theodora and Katina Pavlou resurrect these others and so give him another chance to accept himself. Less austere than Theodora, he gladly takes it and—without losing his faith in illusions as a solace—begins to face his past more squarely:

"Yes," said the General softly. "You, Ludmilla, you are an illusion. You died years ago in the forests of Russia."

She was almost ready to agree.

"Then, thank you, Alyosha Sergei," she said, "thank you for accepting this illusion."

"Oh, illusions are necessary. It is necessary to accept. I shall tell you a secret. Incidentally. I was a major once. Also a colonel. Perhaps."

"Then you have deceived us, *Major*?" Theodora said.

"Deceit, Ludmilla, is a wincing word. I was a general in spirit, always. If I was not in fact, it was due to misfortune, and the superior connexions of my subordinate officers. But how I have lived, in spirit. Such bugles!" (p. 249)

Such bugles! Though Theodora's spirit is more sombre, it does not escape his influence. She would choose, of course, to see Katina Pavlou as Lou Parrott, and not as Varvara. But Sokolnikov knows nothing of Lou Parrott. Guided by him and by her own growing affection for Katina Pavlou, she comes gradually to see Varvara—and hence Fanny—in a more tolerant light. Again, we have seen Theodora's attitude to her mother changing under diverse pressures; but Sokolnikov's amused resistance to Anna Stepanovna's bullying encourages Theodora to regard her mother less earnestly and obsessively.

Through Theodora's being so variously obliged to consider her mother's side of the case, her father has suffered in her esteem. By setting George Goodman in an altered light, Sokolnikov not only redresses this immediate balance but also frees her of a subtler tyranny than ever her mother had imposed. Through Sokolnikov's steady opposition to generalizations about Life and his insistence that circumstances so alter cases that cases cannot intelligibly be divorced from their circumstances, she is given access to a freedom more meaningful than all her cries for Freedom. One complex sequence must serve for all, a sequence that shows also how the quicksilver leaps and shifts of Theodora's fugues match White's purpose as no conventional set of sub-plots or enclosed narratives could possibly have done.

After a hard day as Ludmilla (not to mention Katina's Aunt Smaragda) and a long evening as companion to Elsie van Tuyl, Theodora is greeted, on returning to her room, by a furious quarrel next-door between Wetherby and Lieselotte. She concludes at last that "it is no longer possible . . . to distinguish which is which" (p. 208). Astonished by this new light on her parents' marriage, she tries to compose herself for sleep by reading from *Acts*, a book in which "people came and went with a directness and simplicity that amazed" (p. 208). She dozes in her chair and dreams of reaching Ithaca:

Swimming too, somewhere off the shores of an island, Theodora hitched her trousers under the green water and prepared to touch land. Fire was coming towards her, and voices, and finally heads, along the banks of a little creek.

"Who are you?" they asked, holding their fire close to the water.

"My name is Epaphroditos," said Theodora, rising shakily on sudden stones.

Wind twanged in her moustache, which was thick with salt.

"That is strange," they said. "You are unexpected, to say the least."

"Well, I cannot tell you any more," said Theodora. "Because I am waiting to be told."

Before her stone rolled. She retrieved her head from above her lap in the strict space of her *chambre modeste*.

"You are sleeping, Ludmilla?" asked Alyosha Sergei. (pp. 208-9)

Theodora's dream draws on various sources, bringing together, in one detail or another, Odysseus's actual landing in Ithaca (*Odyssey*, xiii); the account he later gives Eumaeus (xiv); the landing in Phaeacia that leads on to the Nausicaä-episode (v-vi); and Paul's shipwreck on Malta (*Acts*, xxvii-xxviii).

But there is more here than a literary acrostic. In the trouser-hitching, the salt stains, and the stones underfoot there is the force of a certain "actuality". In the trousers of Theodora's mannishness (cf. p. 69) and the moustache of her spinsterhood (cf. pp. 11, 119), this becomes a Theodoran actuality. And, in the swimming in green water (cf. p. 27) and in the fire with which she is greeted (cf. p. 78), there are overtones of sexual fulfilment not Freudian only but also Theodoran.

Theodora, it appears, is landing at last in an Ithaca of her own.[3] As Miss Herring has shown, in the article previously referred to, there are Homeric parallels still later in the novel. But never again, I submit, is Theodora herself in search of Ithaca. From this point on, the more explicit Homeric allusions are directed at Katina Pavlou, who has yet to find herself; and the broad Homeric parallels of Part Three reinforce

---

[3] By virtue of the name she chooses, her recourse to Odysseus's habit of giving false names takes on a finer edge: she is forsaking Athene's patronage in favour of Aphrodite's! This little touch appears to be White's own, for Professor G. P. Shipp tells me that the name "Epaphroditos" was unknown in Homeric Greek and that, even much later, the word remained an adjective meaning "beloved of Aphrodite".

our sense of Theodora's homecoming (such as it is) but do not direct her own.

White is aware, of course, that Theodora must do more than dream that her problems are resolved. When the salt-stained Epaphroditos is accosted by the people of the island, "she" has little to say, "Because I am waiting to be told". The novel's next phrase is "Before her stone rolled": a phrase referring to the landing of Odysseus (*Odyssey*, xiii); a phrase referring to the death of George Goodman (p. 88); and, here in Theodora's *chambre modeste*, a phrase announcing the entry of a drunken Alyosha Sergei.

In the splendid episode that follows, he regales them both with vodka and shares with Theodora the remainder of "their" history. When he tells of encountering the Bolsheviks in a forest-clearing, she imagines the pine-trees and associates them, as always, with her father's presence. As Ludmilla, she does her best to out-face the simple zeal of the revolutionaries:

> "You are answerable to the people."
> "Am I not a person?" asked Theodora.
> "That is not for you to decide." (p. 217)

The decision goes against her. She is shot. And Alyosha Sergei flees:

> "My end was far less apocalyptical," he said. "After a short pause to consider the ethics of it, naturally and regrettably I ran. In the course of this operation I received a slight flesh wound in the left buttock ... But I continued to run." (p. 219)

His whole tale becomes a comic parable and Theodora realizes for the first time that her father was neither the "bearded benevolence" (p. 56) of the church-window at Meroë nor the mere weakling she later saw in him. Less adequate than some of his fellows, he had nevertheless done what he could for her and, far more important, had attended to his own necessities. He had not been Father, but a human being. Theodora has long needed to be shown these things. They can be shown now only because she has at last discovered the compassion, even the good humour, that they deserve.

In the eighty pages that remain of *The Aunt's Story*, there are no further fugues. (The meeting with Holstius in Part

Three is different in kind because he is *entirely* a figment, a fusion of people she has known.) From the point where she accepts Alyosha's flight to the end of the novel, Theodora tries to express the spirit of her new discoveries in altogether more active terms.

There is, to begin with, the affair of the nautilus-shell and the questions of ownership, acquisitiveness, and impossible choice to which it gives rise. When Mrs Rapallo proudly displays her new purchase, Sokolnikov asserts another kind of ownership: " 'It is mine from staring at, for many years. It responded through the glass. A tender, a subtle relationship has existed which now in an instant you destroy' " (p. 164). On that later evening of drunken exhilaration, when he suggests to Theodora that they should " 'look, just once, together, at this lovely shell' " (p. 220), she responds instantly—and predictably—to his more "refined" conception of ownership and gets it from Mrs Rapallo's room. An overwrought Mrs Rapallo appears to reclaim her goods—on the seemingly improbable ground that " 'it is all I have got' " (p. 225)—and Sokolnikov becomes more nakedly possessive. Theodora realizes with dismay that vulgarity is no necessary mark of insincerity, that she must arbitrate between individuals as uncompromising as her parents, and that she cannot do so. When she insists, by turns, that the shell really belongs to each of them, she is told she is drunk. " 'I have never seen more clearly,' said Theodora slowly. 'But what I see remains involved' " (p. 224). This profound truth is no solution. The two struggle over the shell. It is smashed. And "Theodora felt herself considerably reduced" (p. 225).

The sequence of events that brings Part Two to an end begins in a picnic suggested by Katina Pavlou, who is about "to germinate" (p. 233). It is taken up by Theodora with a wry glance into her memory (cf. pp. 58-59), furthered by Wetherby with an ardent glance at Katina Pavlou, and most unenthusiastically received by the others, who feel unsafe beyond their *jardin exotique*. Jealousy makes Lieselotte more savagely bitter than ever. Sokolnikov sulks at first because Katina-Varvara has lately teased him about his age. In the event, his good sense asserts itself and, giving up all amorous pretensions, he begins to treat the girl with a warm, fatherly affection. Meanwhile Theodora feels a strong but rather Olympian concern for them:

> It was necessary that Sokolnikov should feel the final twinge. It was necessary that Katina Pavlou should discover fire. And Theodora Goodman, watching the charade move with all the hopes and hesitations of the human mechanism, knew that because she loved and pitied, the humiliation and the pain were also necessarily hers. (p. 238)

She is hardly the Theodora who felt that "there is no life-line to other lives" (p. 137). But she still does not recognize the extent of her involvement. When the time comes for Katina Pavlou to "discover fire", she herself will "feel the final twinge" as sharply as Sokolnikov. In this "charade" she is an actor.

His plans of seduction frustrated at the picnic, Wetherby later arranges to meet Katina Pavlou at the tower along the coast. Sensing Theodora's opposition, he frankly tells her of his intention, implies that Katina is sexually experienced, and impugns Theodora's motives: " 'Perhaps in different circumstances I would have lain with my head in your lap, and discussed Tennyson and Morris. But the escalators have carried us apart' " (p. 245). Although Theodora's only objection is to Wetherby personally, she is shaken by his attack and characteristically inclined to accept this perversion of her motives. She is further rebuffed by the joyfully unapproachable music that Katina Pavlou plays before setting out.

Yet Theodora finds the strength of purpose to consult Sokolnikov, only to be met with an air of indifference. Unable to believe that he could speak so if he were aware of *these* circumstances, she is horrified to find that he knows very well:

> "They have taken the coast road," he said. "They are walking towards the tower which has some connexion with Napoleon. He has taken her hand because she expects him to. And although his hand is dead, she is moved, because the music is still moving in her own. It does not matter much whether it is he. Because she has chosen. She has chosen this as the moment of experience. And experience has a glaze. It has not yet *cracked*," the General almost shouted. (p. 249)

Beneath the insistence that no rescue is necessary, there lies a dismayed belief that no rescue is possible. Made obvious by his last phrase, Alyosha Sergei's dismay manifests itself also in his imposition on himself of a quite uncharacteristic flatness of tone. Although Theodora does not know it, he is indeed feeling "the final twinge" of losing Varvara once more and of losing, too, his new-found daughter.

Unable to stir him, Theodora sets out alone. She is too late for any melodramatic rescue and at first, indeed, she is rebuffed. But gradually she and Katina begin to talk, only a little indirectly, of what has happened:

"Have you ever been inside the tower, Miss Goodman?" Katina Pavlou asked ...

"No," said Theodora, "I have not been inside the tower. I imagine there is very little to see."

"There is nothing, nothing," Katina said. "There is a smell of rot and emptiness."

But no less painful in its emptiness, Theodora felt.

"Still, I am glad," said Katina Pavlou, speaking through her white face. "You know, Miss Goodman, when one is glad for something that has happened, something nauseating and painful, that one did not suspect. It is better finally to know." (pp. 252-53)

The Aunt's Story is not a novel where attitudes are either totally "endorsed" or else dismissed outright. If Theodora's new faith in rescues has proved too crude, Sokolnikov's aloofness, notwithstanding its cost to him, is yet not subtle enough. For Theodora's little solaces are more valuable that she supposes. She takes "the cold, dead hand, that she would begin to warm" (p. 252). She talks of small things and listens to bigger ones while the girl recovers her bearings. And, later that evening, she responds sympathetically to a growing mood of fulfilment:

There were lamps and candles. There was the legendary light of oil and wax. There was the light of light . . . The eyelids on Katina Pavlou's face were still and golden. (p. 253)

This mood of fulfilment may suggest that the middle-aged doubts and fears of Theodora and Alyosha Sergei are more or less ironically rendered and that the novel comes down at last on the side of life, testifying to such healthful aphorisms as "A connection each day keeps the death-wish at bay". And, indeed, such a thesis would not be without grounds. Katina Pavlou's insistence that, despite both pain and unpleasantness, "it is better finally to know" echoes Theodora's youthful determination to know all the implications of experience, including sexual experience.

Such a thesis, however, is too simple to meet the novel's persistent emphasis on circumstance. For all its cost to her, Theodora's rejection of the particular suitors who presented themselves to her was well-advised. And now, following immediately on the sight of Katina Pavlou still and golden in the light of consummation, we are to hear some squalid truths about Mrs Rapallo's sexual history. Theodora finds her contemplating suicide from sheer weariness of her existence and of the romantic fictions that have long been its only support. The dark, mysterious Rapallo of Theodora's imaginings had, in fact, been a man who came to her door one Thursday morning " 'selling a patent medicine. He undressed me with his eyes. I was not unwilling. I had fallen for his boots and his sadness. I fell. I fell. . . . I came to ten years later,' she said, 'on an iron bedstead, in a cheap hotel in Munich. All he had left behind was a pair of yellow gloves' " (p. 256). Throughout her tenuous career since then, Gloria has been her chief consolation, being " 'unlike any child of the bowels, entirely mine' " (p. 255). Her secret is out at last: " 'It is time, Theodora Goodman, that you and I agreed that the Principessa does not exist' " (p. 255).

Since Mrs Rapallo has been the mere slave of her illusions, there seems little virtue in Theodora's persuading her to leave her sleeping-tablets alone and to try to face her life. And yet, when the hotel catches fire that night, Theodora's persuasions bear good fruit. With nothing whatever to live for, Mrs Rapallo is fortunate at least in the splendid death, her glory apparent to all eyes, with which Theodora has unwittingly presented her:

The window had become quite encrusted with fire. It had a considerable, stiff jewelled splendour of its own, that ignored the elaborate ritual of the flames. Everything else, the whole night, was subsidiary to this ritual of fire . . .

[It] was obvious that Mrs Rapallo was gratified by such magnificence. From the window she contemplated, only vaguely, the vague evidence of faces. Fire is fiercer. Fire is more triumphant. Then, she turned and withdrew, and there was the windowful of smoke . . . (pp. 261-62)

Before Theodora joins the survivors—Katina Pavlou, Grigg, Sokolnikov, and the Blochs—she has a last encounter with Lieselotte, who had started the fire by throwing a lamp at Wetherby. Unable to find him in their blazing room, Lieselotte desperately calls Theodora to help in the search: "Terror was streaming in her wax hair. But Theodora's gestures were wood. She watched the revival of roses, how they glowed, glowing and blowing like great clusters of garnets on the live hedge" (p. 259). Theodora is perfectly willing to help. But she is distracted for too long a moment by recollections of her mother and of Meroë—the garnets and the roses. While she is recovering her mother's ring, Lieselotte disappears into the smoke and does not return. When Theodora finds herself outside with the others, she

. . . put the garnet ring on its usual finger, below the joint which showed signs of stiffening with arthritis. It was rather an ugly little ring, but part of the flesh. In the presence of the secret, leaping emotions of the fire she was glad to have her garnet. (p. 260)

An ugly little ring, but part of the flesh: Theodora has at last come to terms with her mother. Borne on by the force of this discovery, she gives herself up to thoughts of Meroë. Europe has done its work, the *jardin exotique* survives but no longer threatens, and, in a wave of nostalgia, Part Two comes to an end.

The wave recedes, as it must, for the past not only lies beyond direct access but has even intruded on the present in a way she finds intolerable. Even while she was searching for the ring, she was neglecting a direct appeal for help. And, being Theodora, she allows herself no credit at all for the less tangible things we have seen her doing for Mrs Rapallo, Katina Pavlou, and Sokolnikov. Being Theodora, that is to say, she still cannot recognize her own need to be judged with the compassion she bestows so generously on others. Her assaults on her one remaining enemy, her attempts to extinguish every vestige of "the great monster Self" (p. 134) lie at the heart of the brief

American sojourn that makes up Part Three. Only when these issues are resolved can the novel reach a true ending.

The turning-point of this last phase of the novel comes when Theodora encounters Holstius, who gives Part Three its name.[4] He bears marks enough of father-figures in general and of George Goodman and Alyosha Sergei in particular to indicate that, unlike the actors in Theodora's fugues, he is entirely an emanation of her *psyche*. At bottom Holstius is Theodora herself drawing on her experience of fatherly preceptors in order to act as preceptor to herself. When "he" persuades her of something which those others had striven to teach her, we are to recognize that she is at last assimilating the earlier lesson.

On his first visit, he obliges her to accept that she cannot extinguish her identity and need not even wish to do so. Long ago Theodora had discovered that, by killing her mother, she would, among other things, cut herself off from the memories that give anyone's life much of its meaning. Not until now does she see that the extinction of the great monster Self will exact the same price. Only now does she give up her quest for the "freedom" of perfect inanition; and, by doing so, she gains a new and altered access to her memories of those whom she had cherished and some whom she had not:

... there was no end to the lives of Theodora Goodman. These met and parted, met and parted, movingly. They entered into each other, so that the impulse for music in Katina Pavlou's hands, and the steamy exasperation of Sokolnikov, and Mrs Rapallo's baroque and narcotized despair were the same and understandable. And in the same way that the created lives of Theodora Goodman were interchangeable, the lives into which she had entered, making them momentarily dependent for love or hate, owing her this portion of their fluctuating personalities, whether George or Julia Goodman, only apparently deceased, or Huntly Clarkson, or Moraïtis, or Lou, or Zack, these were the lives of Theodora Goodman, these too. (pp. 299-300)

When Holstius returns next morning, it is to tell her that, as she has foreseen, the strangers into whose hands she has

---

[4] His own name, I take it, is a Latinization of *holz*, expressive of his relationship to George Goodman: "She looked through the trees for the tree walking, which in time would become Holstius." (p. 294)

fallen are convinced of her madness and propose to lock her up. The only course open to her, he maintains, is an outward submission coupled with an inward self-respect. On these terms and these alone is freedom possible even for a prisoner. Accordingly, when they do come for her, she lets pass as pointless a clear opportunity to escape. And then, in the last sentences of the novel, through motifs that fully support the weight placed on them, it is made plain that Theodora Goodman has achieved a genuine freedom. As Holstius had suggested, she restores to its place the last surviving token of the identity she had tried to extinguish: "The hat sat straight, but the doubtful rose trembled and glittered, leading a life of its own." (p. 303).

To the brutally obtuse Frank Parrott, " 'Theo has always led her own life' " (p. 271). We, on the other hand, share her knowledge of her years of servitude and of her later struggles. The last sentence of all proclaims her ultimate success. She, too, is a doubtful rose: but she is now capable, whatever her circumstances, of leading a life of her own.

3/1966

Visions of the Mandala in
The Tree of Man

A. P. RIEMER

I

Both the title and the explicit concerns of *The Solid Mandala*, as Miss T. G. Herring has noted,[1] declare unambiguously the use of a body of mystical and visionary material derived from the writings and observations of Carl Jung. From the case histories of patients with neurotic and psychotic disorders, Jung formulated his theory based on the concept of the mandala, that symbol or image of divine perfection and transcendental harmony which man conjures in his dreams to articulate his longing for religious experience. Jung's studies of the iconography of much European and Eastern art and the *allegoriae* or visions of Christian mystics enabled him to chart the development and mutation of the mandala-experience, and the concept soon developed into a corner-stone of the much more extensive theory of the archetypes of the collective unconscious.

Arthur Brown's brightly-coloured marbles, his solid mandalas, are for him symbols of absolute perfection, concentrated embodiments of the fullness and richness of life he has been able to attain and which he tries to communicate to others.

However many marbles Arthur had—there were always those which got lost, and some he traded for other things—he considered four his permanencies. There were the speckled gold and the cloudy blue. There was the whorl of green and crimson circlets. There was the taw with a knot at the centre, which made him consider palming it off, until, on looking long and close, he dis-

[1] "Self and Shadow: The Quest for Totality in *The Solid Mandala*", pp. 72-82 above.

covered the knot was the whole point. Of all those jewels or touchstones, talismans or sweethearts, Arthur Brown got to love the knotted one best, and for staring at it, and rubbing at it, should have seen his face inside.[2]

These objects, treasured and hoarded by Arthur, the Browns' apparently subnormal son, seem at first sight chosen at random, meaningful only to his private and eccentric imagination. But they illustrate very closely some of Jung's observations concerning religious symbolism, especially in its manifestations in mandalic dreams and visions. Arthur's marbles are four in number: one is blue, the other gold; the third contains a combination of crimson and green while the fourth, most treasured by him, has no distinguishing colour but is identified by its knot. The number of these objects, their shape and the colours contained in them help us to identify them with two notions that loom large in Jung's discussions of religious symbolism: the quaternity and the alchemic notion of the philosopher's stone. Jung mentions constantly that his patients experienced dreams of an obviously religious nature in which the number four (or multiples of four) featured with remarkable consistency, even though, as he points out, the symbolic number in Christian religious experience is three (denoting the Trinity). Jung argues that four is a much more potent and meaningful number than three in religious mysticism, and he connects its importance with the age-old pursuit of the perfect, primal matter, the philosopher's stone which not only possesses the quality of transmuting base matter into gold, but can, also, reveal to its finder the secrets of divinity. Moreover, the concept of quaternity according to Jung is closely connected with the alchemic problem of squaring the circle, which, in turn, was supposed to lead to the discovery of the philosopher's stone.

The image of the circle—regarded as the most perfect form since Plato's *Timaeus*, the prime authority for Hermetic philosophy— was assigned to the most perfect substance, to the gold, also to the *anima mundi* or *anima media natura*, and to the first created light. And because the macrocosm, the Great World, was made by the creator "in a form round and globose", the smallest part of the whole, the point, also possesses this perfect nature . . . This

[2] *The Solid Mandala* (London, 1966), p. 228. All page references are to this edition.

image of the Deity dormant and concealed in matter was what the alchemists called the original chaos, or the earth of paradise, or the round fish in the sea, or the egg, or simply the *rotundum*. That round thing was in possession of the magical key which unlocked the closed doors of matter. As is said in the *Timaeus*, only the demiurge, the perfect being, is capable of dissolving the tetraktys, the embrace of the four elements.[3]

For Arthur Brown, therefore, the knotted taw is the *rotundum* which contains the secrets of the universe; moreover, Arthur seems to be the demiurge who could unlock its secrets, except that he cannot recognize his own image reflected in it (if I read White's rather paradoxical statement correctly).

In another passage, Jung explains the nature of the demiurge who possesses the powers that Arthur seems capable of possessing:

From the Latin treatises it is also evident that the latent demiurge, dormant and concealed in matter, is identical with the so-called *homo philosophicus*, the second Adam. He is the spiritual man, Adam Kadmon, often identified with Christ. Whereas the original Adam was mortal, because he was made of the corruptible four elements, the second Adam is immortal, because he consists of one pure and incorruptible essence. Thus Pseudo-Thomas says: "The second Adam passed from the pure elements into eternity. Therefore, since he consists of simple and pure essence he endures forever." (p. 55)

It seems to me evident that in the twin brothers Arthur and Waldo Brown White is following this duality, described by Jung, of the two Adams or original men, one divine in his purity, the other mortal and corruptible. Arthur's discovery of his solid mandalas appears to give him the ability of becoming this demiurge and knowing the ultimate secret of life. But though Arthur loves the knotted, apparently colourless mandala best, he recognizes that it is not, ultimately, for him "Because this rather confusing oddity was really not his own. His seemed more the coil of green and crimson circlets" (p. 228). If this passage is to be understood, we must recognize the knotted marble as the philosopher's stone, the true *rotundum*, while the other three are merely contributory to it, and in his choice of one of these others, Arthur unconsciously declares

[3] C. G. Jung, *Psychology and Religion* (*Collected Works* Vol. XI, pp. 53-54). All quotations from Jung refer to this volume.

that, while he possesses the potentiality of being Adam Kadmon, he will not unlock the secrets of immutable matter. It is the other mandala which Arthur retains at the end of the novel after losing the knotted one:

> Only when reduced to nothing he remembered that one mandala must be left, and rummaged through the other contents of his pockets. The first and sleaziest ray of light from the entrance to the lane showed him the whorled marble lying in the hollow of his hand. The knotted mandala was the one he had lost. (p. 307)

That Arthur has not become the demiurge, that the whorled marble is not the true philosopher's stone, that Arthur loses the true one, can seem wild conjectures, but I believe that if we take into account the peculiar colour symbolism Jung constantly associates with the quaternity and mandalic experiences, the author's intention becomes quite clear.

In *Psychology and Religion,* Jung discusses two mandalic experiences widely separated in time: one was the dreams of a young man he treated for psychotic disorders, the other a poem by the fourteenth-century mystic Guillaume de Deguileville. Jung found that there was a certain similarity in the quaternary colours seen by Guillaume in his mystic vision of heaven and by his patient in the reported dream. The patient saw four colours: gold, red, blue and green; Guillaume in his vision looks up at a golden heaven, and becomes aware "of a small circle, only three feet wide and of the colour of sapphire", and "the blue circle was rolling like a disc upon a great circle which intersected the golden sphere of the heaven" (p. 68). Jung therefore notes that in Guillaume's vision there are two systems, one golden and one blue, just as his patient dreamt of two such systems, "the vertical circle is blue, and the horizontal one containing four colours is golden" (p. 67). Jung conjectures that in both visions the golden circle denotes the heavens, the abode of the Father, while the blue is a symbol of time, or the "ecclesiastical calendar". Two of Arthur's marbles are "cloudy blue" and "speckled gold" respectively in colour. These correspond, then, to the two separate systems in both visions described in *Psychology and Religion,* and it is notable that among Arthur's four marbles, the gold and the blue are distinguished because they consist only of colours, whereas the other two, the red and green whorled and the knotty taw, are distinguished more by their inner shapes. At this point, the similarity between Guillaume's poem and the patient's dream begins to break down. The patient has a clear insight of the four colours, blue, gold, red and green. But when Guillaume questions an angel about the mystery of the Trinity, the angel informs him that God created three colours, red, green and gold. Jung notes that the fourth principal colour (blue) symbolizing the Mother of God, the essential female spirit is missing from the angel's account, whereas Guillaume himself sees it clearly in the early part of the vision. Jung conjectures that this is brought about through the conflict in Guillaume's mind between the trinitarian doctrine of the Church and the essential archetypal quaternity of religious experience as revealed in dreams and visions. Jung's patient, not recognizing the religious and ecclesiastical nature of his dreams, was not troubled by the paradox that causes Guillaume to be distressed about the nature of the Trinity (when he has an intrinsic sense that four is the normal harmonic disposition of colours) and this in turn leads his angelic informant into an uncommunicative taciturnity. "Three there are, but where is the fourth?" Jung quotes Plato (p. 70) to demonstrate the disjunction in Guillaume's vision and to show, at the same time, the mysterious intuition of perfection the union of four colours brings about.

A similar disjunction occurs in the disposition of Arthur's marbles. The four colours are contained in three of them, with Arthur's own combining two of the colours; the fourth, the presumably perfect but elusive mandala, is apparently colourless. It seems to me that in this White demonstrates Jung's thesis that a modern mandalic vision, while approaching the perfection of a classically orthodox experience, differs from it through modern man's inability to project an image of God, to find a notion of divinity apart from himself and his existence. The red and green marble is closer to the colourless, perfect one than the other two. It consists of two colours and a whorled shape, whereas the others are merely coloured. The shape inside the red and green marble is described as whorled, and presumably it is therefore less compact and less complex than the *knotted* shape inside the colourless one. Similarly, the whorled marble has two distinct colours, but the other being colourless contains, it seems, a perfect resolution of the four colours which produces whiteness, or more precisely the absence of colour.

In this way I would suggest that for White the lost mandala symbolizes the equivalent of the philosopher's stone or the *rotundum*, and Arthur's choice of the marble nearest to it in complexity of colour and design suggests that although he is able to approach perfection more closely than anyone else in the novel, finality will necessarily elude him. This, in Jungian terms, seems the predicament of modern man unable to project the notion of divinity. At one stage in the novel, Arthur reads in an encyclopaedia a definition of the mandala derived from Jung, as Miss Herring notes:

"The Mandala is a symbol of totality. It is believed to be the 'dwelling of the god'. Its protective circle is a pattern of order superimposed on—psychic—chaos. Sometimes its geometric form is seen as a vision . . . " (p. 238)

Later, Arthur questions his father about "the meaning of 'totality' ", but he is rebuffed with empty platitudes.

Then Arthur realized Dad would never know, any more than Waldo. It was himself who was, and would remain, the keeper of mandalas, who must guess their final secret through touch and light. (p. 240)

But the novel's irony is that Arthur never guesses the final secret of the mandalas because he cannot recognize his own face reflected in the most perfect one. Arthur is not the demiurge; if anyone in the novel approaches that status it is his friend Mrs Poulter. The lost mandala is never recovered; yet illogically it is suggested that Mrs Poulter, with her ability to respond to Arthur the dill, might become the demiurge, as well as the mysterious anima mentioned so often by Jung in connection with the visions and dreams he discusses. Arthur gives her the gold mandala after he performs the mandala dance for her; a little earlier he had given the blue one to Dulcie just before her wedding to Leonard Saporta. It is clear therefore that the two simpler marbles go to the two women; the knotted one he offers to Waldo, despite his misgivings that

Waldo "would never be able to untie the knot". This is Arthur's great mistake: Waldo cannot experience a mandalic vision; Arthur, possibly, could have achieved a full one, but his love for his brother causes him to offer Waldo the perfect marble.

Subsequently the marble is lost. Possibly it will never be found, though the end of the novel suggests to me, irrationally I stress, that unwittingly Mrs Poulter is to be the custodian of this symbol of perfection. This seems to me to be so because of another point the novel seems to be making about Arthur's failure to achieve the highest visionary state. He (like the novel) is conscious of the nature and meaning of a mandalic experience, and recurrently in White's novels it is stressed that self-consciousness (indeed articulateness itself) is damaging and destructive. Mrs Poulter knows nothing about mandalas, for her they are merely childish marbles which Arthur the dill treasures, but unlike the arid Waldo she sympathizes with Arthur's dedication to these trivial and unmanly objects.

There is a further reason why Arthur cannot achieve visionary fulfilment. I would suggest that the mysterious fourth mandala is potent for him only while it exists in a quaternity with the other three which display the four principal colours. Arthur's goodness, his saintliness, makes him give away his most treasured possessions, and while this clearly establishes his worth and humanity, it means that, with tragic irony, he denies himself the ability of becoming divine. At the end he repudiates his visions; the repudiation is an act of supreme charity, but personally, for Arthur, its consequences are tragic.

II

The symbolism attached to Arthur's enigmatic marbles by no means exhausts the wealth of Jungian references in *The Solid Mandala*—the dance of the mandala, which Arthur performs for Mrs Poulter, is but one of a number of such references which are quite explicit in their significance. I do not propose to examine the novel further because my main concern is to demonstrate that while these things are explicit in this novel (indeed they are overt in the consciousness of the central character), such material also features in the earlier ones. I am restricting myself to an examination of a portion of

The Tree of Man which seems to bear a very close affinity to such Jungian material, though I have no doubt that the material is used in other works as well, especially in *Riders in the Chariot*. My main contention is that in *The Tree of Man* White relies implicitly on this material without bringing it specifically into the conceptual framework of the novel, as he does in *The Solid Mandala*, yet its recognition is equally important for the comprehension of his intentions. A novelist's use of such arcane material will inevitably involve questions of propriety: but I prefer to leave this problem of artistic licence to be fought out elsewhere, as I have no doubt it will be. I am intent only on demonstrating the dependence of the novel on certain experiences described and formulated by Jung; I would stress that I am not offering specific sources, since I feel that White's reading of Jung is more extensive than mine, and that he has absorbed rather than translated this material. The points of reference I use are taken from *Psychology and Religion* and I find this advantageous because it would have been accessible to White when engaged on writing *The Tree of Man*.

In Chapter 25 of *The Tree of Man* Stan Parker sustains his most intense (and for the reader most perplexing) vision. By this stage of the novel the world of the Parkers has been almost completely destroyed; the tract of virgin country they had settled and tamed at the beginning of the book has been taken over by the soulless incursions of suburbia, and their "place" has become an eccentric enclave amid the texture-brick of a large metropolis. Their daughter Thelma has made a compromise with society in marrying her employer, a successful lawyer, and at the beginning of this chapter she is glimpsed living a vicarious and arid life by responding to the artificial stimulus provided by a concert. Their son Ray had refused to make Thelma's compromise, and he was ostracized from society: he ended his life by being murdered in a shabby, drunken brawl. Thus the Parkers' world has collapsed around them, and both the husband and wife have retreated into themselves and seem to be preparing for the final spiritual annihilation. It is then that Stan suffers a cerebral stroke which seems to rob him of the last remaining vestige of stature and integrity. It is in this desperate and apparently destroyed state that Stan experiences his most magnificent vision of totality.

The vision begins in an atmosphere of meditative relaxation:

> That afternoon the old man's chair had been put on the grass at the back, which was quite dead-looking from the touch of winter. Out there at the back, the grass, you could hardly call it a lawn, had formed a circle in the shrubs and trees which the old woman had not so much planted as stuck in during her lifetime. There was little of design in the garden originally, though one had formed out of the wilderness. It was perfectly obvious that the man was seated at the heart of it, and from this heart the trees radiated, with grave movements of life, and beyond them the sweep of a vegetable garden, which had gone to weed during the months of the man's illness, presented the austere skeletons of cabbages and the wands of onion seed. All was circumference to the centre, and beyond that the worlds of other circles, whether crescent of purple villas or the bare patches of earth, on which rabbits sat and observed some abstract spectacle for minutes on end, in a paddock not yet built upon. The last circle but one was the cold and golden bowl of winter, enclosing all that was visible and material, and at which the man would blink from time to time, out of his watery eyes, unequal to the effort of realizing he was the centre of it.[4]

Several important points must be noted about this passage dealing with the commencement of Stan's mystical experience. He is seated at the centre of a vast series of concentric circles, beginning with the garden and its radiating trees, and then extending to the last circle but one, "the cold and golden bowl of winter". White presents Stan as becoming slowly aware of his experience: at first he is totally unaware of it, but by the end he recognizes the tremendousness of what is happening to him, even though he is "unequal to the effort of realizing that he was the centre of it". Moreover, White stresses that this symmetry and design Stan now perceives were not always obvious, and, most important of all, that Amy had never intended that the trees and shrubs planted erratically throughout a lifetime should form a circle around the patch of grass where her husband is sitting.

[4] *The Tree of Man* (London, 1956), pp. 493-94. All quotations are from this edition.

It is clear, therefore, that in this ordinary and familiar setting Stan Parker experiences a mandalic vision; he feels that he is at the centre—indeed he becomes the centre—of a series of circles which had formed mysteriously from his random and apparently asymmetrical environment. The following statement by Jung is relevant:

Historically, as we have seen, the mandala served as a symbol to clarify the nature of the deity philosophically, or to represent the same thing in a visible form for the purpose of adoration, or, as in the East, as a yantra for yoga practices. The wholeness ("perfection") of the celestial circle and the squareness of the earth, combining the four principles or elements or psychic qualities, express completeness and union. Thus the mandala has the status of a "uniting symbol". (p. 79)

Obviously, Stan's experience in his backyard is in many ways similar to Jung's formulation, though there are important differences which must be examined presently. Stan's experience of perfection, wholeness and unity is not complete because he does not see beyond "the last circle but one". Curiously enough, while three of the Jungian colours are alluded to in his vision, the fourth, blue, remains unseen. In the first place White stresses the greenness of Stan's immediate surroundings, not through colour sensations but through concentration on the vegetation—the grass, shrubs, trees, cabbages and so on. Beyond these red appears in the "purple villas" which can only refer to the reddish texture-brick White dislikes so much. This is contained by the "cold and golden bowl" of winter—beyond that Stan cannot see, and I would suggest that it is infinity, the most extreme expression of time, and therefore connected with the colour blue (as in Jung's patient's dream and in Guillaume's vision) which Stan is not yet privileged to witness.

At this point, Stan's vision is disturbed by what seems like a gratuitously grotesque interruption:

The large, triumphal scheme of which he was becoming mysteriously aware made him shift in his seat, and resent the entrance of the young man, who had jumped the fence and was coming down towards him, stepping over beds rather than following paths, he was so convinced of achieving his mission by direct means and approaches.

> Stan Parker was shrinking all this time. He did not like to speak to people now. His skin was papery, you could see through it almost in certain light. His eyes had been reduced to a rudimentary shape, through which was observed, you felt, a version of objects that was possibly true. (p. 494)

This rude incursion into Stan's visionary privacy is by a young man possessing the full fervour of evangelical zeal. He unfolds a lurid tale of his former sinfulness "Drinking and whoring most week-ends . . . There were black women too". He then quizzes Stan about the state of his soul and offers him tracts and pamphlets which invite him to salvation.

> The evangelist smiled with youthful incredulity. No subtleties would escape the steam roller of faith. "You don't understand," he said smilingly.
> If you can understand, at your age, what I have been struggling with all my life, then it is a miracle, thought the old man.
> He spat on the ground in front of him. He had been sitting for some time in one position, and had on his chest a heaviness of phlegm.
> "I am too old," he said colourlessly.
> He was tired really. He wanted to be left alone.
> "But the glories of salvation," persisted the evangelist, whose hair went up in even waves, "these great glories are everybody's for the asking, just by a putting out of the hand."
> The old man fidgeted. He was not saying anything. Great glories were glittering in the afternoon. He had already been a little dazzled.
> "You are not stubborn, friend?"
> "I would not be here if I was not stubborn," said the old man.
> "Don't you believe in God, perhaps?" asked the evangelist, who had begun to look around him and to feel the necessity for some further stimulus of confession. "I can show you books," he yawned.
> Then the old man, who had been cornered long enough, saw, through perversity perhaps, but with his own eyes. He was illuminated.
> He pointed with his stick at the gob of spittle.
> "That is God," he said.
> As it lay glittering intensely and personally on the ground. (p. 495)

It is obvious from this passage, without recourse to any exotic material, that the young evangelist is brought on to the scene to allow Stan to discover for himself an intensely private intuition of divinity which has nothing to do with the conventional formulations of organized religion. Discovering God in a gob of spittle is man's confirmation of his own divinity, and Stan recognizes in his own excretion a private but splendid clue to the meaning of life. Yet, I would argue, Jung's ideas about modern (as opposed to classical) visions of the mandala illuminate this passage and explain specifically a meaning which is merely implicit and suggested. Jung discovered an all-important difference between the mandalic visions of modern man and those recorded in the literature and art of former epochs. The difference is this:

Prejudiced by historical analogies, we would expect a deity to occupy the centre of the mandala. The centre is, however, empty ... The centre, as a rule, is emphasized. But what we find there is a symbol with a very different meaning. It is a star, a sun, a flower, a cross with equal arms, a precious stone, a bowl filled with water or wine, a serpent coiled up, or a human being, but never a god. (p. 80)

It follows that:

A modern mandala is an involuntary confession of a peculiar mental condition. There is no deity in the mandala, nor is there any submission or reconciliation to a deity. The place of the deity seems to be taken by the wholeness of man. (p. 82)

Stan Parker thus discovers his own divinity, and thereby confirms his being a modern man: it is his own spittle, formed into what I would like to call the nearly solid mandala of a gob, that allows him to complete his vision, to penetrate into the finality and totality that had eluded him until the intrusion of organized religion in the form of the young evangelist. Now he is able to perceive that man must find in himself his own divinity, his own and very private grandeur. And this is later confirmed in *The Solid Mandala* when Mrs Poulter realizes that Arthur's humanity makes him more than divine (p. 303).

But throughout his writings Jung stresses the danger of this egocentricity in modern man who is no longer able to believe in the old formulations of the numinous; his science and his Cartesianism persuade him that all the secrets of the universe can be unlocked with his own intellect. This is connected specifically with modern scepticism concerning the psyche, or religious experience in general, and Jung's thesis can be summarized as claiming that since mankind has attempted to view the whole of life in rational, *conscious* terms, the inevitable manifestations of the psyche lead to neuroses and indeed to tremendous upheavals of the human tribe, because the protective walls of dogma, belief and superstition have been completely demolished. The mandala vision, however, is the psyche's own way of establishing these protective enclosures, just as the orthodox mandalic representations protected the gods contained within them.

The experience formulated by the modern mandala is typical of people who cannot project the divine image any longer. Owing to the withdrawal and introjection of the image they are in danger of inflation and dissociation of personality. The round or square enclosures built round the centre therefore have the purpose of protective walls or of a *vas hermeticum*, to prevent an outburst or a disintegration. Thus the mandala denotes and assists exclusive concentration on the centre, the self. This is anything but egocentricity. On the contrary, it is a much needed self-control for the purpose of avoiding inflation and dissociation. (p. 95)

This is one of the reasons why White seems to me to be so careful to establish the notion of the bankruptcy of conventional religious dogmas just at the moment when Stan's vision of perfection rises to its climax. Modern man, he seems to argue, cannot project the divine image, he must find it within himself, in his gobs of spittle or solid mandalas, those philosopher's stones where he *can* see his own image reflected, just as Stan appears to recognize his own divine image inside his own excretion. He is therefore protected. Stan's vision is, indeed, not egocentric, though he is at the centre of it, because he is able to establish an empathy and a harmony between himself and his material surroundings. His self is not destroyed as the evangelist's (who is the epitome of modernity) has been destroyed by the stultifying effects of society and outmoded dogmas; he has an intuition of the wholeness of man.

Yet there is always the danger of inflation. After the evangelist leaves, Amy comes on the scene to demonstrate the spiritual plight of those who cannot glimpse their own protective mandalas:

> After he had gone and the tracts were flapping and plapping in the undergrowth, and the black dog had smelled one with the tip of his dry nose, the old man continued to stare at the jewel of spittle. A great tenderness of understanding rose in his chest. Even the most obscure, the most sickening incidents of his life were clear. In that light. How long will they leave me like this, he wondered, in peace and understanding?
> But his wife had to come presently.
> "Stan," she said, approaching, he knew it was she, crunching over the grass with her bad leg, "you will not believe when I tell you," she said, "I was scratching round the shack, in the weed, where the rosebush was that we moved to the house, the old white rose, and what did I find, Stan, but the little silver nutmeg grater that Mrs Erbey gave me on our wedding day. Look." (pp. 495-96)

Amy's inflation, her egocentricity, her inability to see beyond the material world, is symbolized by the recovery of this useless though beautiful object. She does, indeed, suffer from the condition of modern man, and this has forced her into a possessiveness which White presents throughout the latter parts of the novel as destructive and stultifying. She had tried to possess her children and ruined them in consequence; she had tried, also, to possess her husband, but he had always eluded her, and is, finally, to elude her once more. At the moment of death, Stan Parker, the lean old man, is able to escape his wife and her possessiveness, while the inflated Amy (it is notable how often her bulk and his spareness are contrasted in this chapter) remains behind, trying, as always, to drag him back to her material level.

At the moment of his death, Stan's quaternary vision is complete: he has a glimpse of the blue sky with its golden sun, and his achievement is triumphant:

> I believe, he said, in the cracks in the path. On which ants were massing, struggling up over an escarpment. But struggling. Like the painful sun in the icy sky. Whirling and whirling. But struggling. But joyful. So much so, he was trembling. The sky was blurred now. As he stood waiting for the flesh to be loosened on him, he prayed for greater clarity, and it became obvious as a

hand. It was clear that One, and no other figure, is the answer to all sums. (p. 497)

Arthur's question, "what is totality" is, therefore, answered by Stan Parker in this earlier novel. He, not Arthur, unlocks the secret of the philosopher's stone; he escapes the bondage of flesh in which, even now, his wife struggles to entrap him:

"Stan," cried his wife, running, because she really was afraid that she had been left behind.

They clung together for a minute on the broken concrete path, their two souls wrestling together. She would have dragged him back if she could, to share her further sentence, which she could not contemplate for that moment, except in terms of solitary confinement. So she was holding him with all the strength of her body and her will. But he was escaping from her.

"Ahhhhhh," she cried when he was lying on the path.

Looking at him.

He could not tell her she would not find it in his face. She was already too far.

"It is all right," he said.

She was holding his head and looking into it some minutes after there was anything left to see. (p. 497)

III

There are a number of other passages in *The Tree of Man* where White appears to me to be relying on a similar body of material for much of his meaning—a fairly significant one is the fire in the Armstrongs' house when Stan rescues the captive Madeleine—but this final vision and experience seem to me to sum up perfectly the author's reliance on Jungian formulations. I feel that it is not sufficient merely to chart the extent of this reliance or to demonstrate how it helps to elucidate the significance of certain passages: I would argue that White employs this material because its assumptions happen perfectly to fit his own views and preoccupations which have little to do, ultimately, with Jung's somewhat bizarre notions.

The main concerns of White's novels have been rehearsed in a number of places with great thoroughness: his affinity with Lawrence, especially in his deep-seated suspicion of modern suburban life with its spiritually stultifying effects, has been noted, as has another literary affinity, a penchant for the divine fool, the Dostoevskian outcast who is ostracized by society at large and yet is capable of feelings and experiences which are magnificent though finally limited in the face of society's hostility and indifference. Increasingly in the novels (and other works) the spurned, the stunted and the disabled, those who dwell on the fringes of society or beyond it, gain White's sympathy and dedication, and Arthur Brown is quite obviously the distillation of this tendency which is represented in *The Tree of Man* by Bub Quigley, and by others before him. Arthur Brown, specifically, seems to bear a close affinity to Prince Myshkin of *The Idiot*, since both characters possess an almost divine saintliness (Mrs Poulter thinks of Arthur in Christ-like terms at the end of *The Solid Mandala*), yet even in the earlier novel this preoccupation is very much in evidence.

It is in these outcasts, in people alienated from society and all but the most limited contacts with humanity, that White finally discovers the resolution to the spiritual paralysis he sees everywhere in modern society. Man must, he argues, be destroyed materially before he is able to ascend to a visionary height of achievement which liberates his soul, which allows him that intuition of infinity that is the clue to life. It seems to me an epitome of White's pessimism about the possibilities of life in the modern world that in his latest novel the possessor of this should be as severely limited as Arthur is. *The Tree of Man* offers a contrast with the later novel in this respect. Stan, too, is stunted: the novel has charted his destruction by society, and it has also conferred on him the symbolic disability of a cerebral stroke; moreover, it is only at the end of his life, a few minutes before his death, that Stan is able to rise to the apex of his visionary achievement. And yet it is he who is given this experience, not the divine idiot, Bub Quigley, nor even Mr Gage, the husband of the postmistress whom Amy discovers in a curious yoga-like attitude contemplating ants. This is important, because even at the end of his life Stan is still closer to recognizable, mundane reality than other visionaries and, most important of all, his achievement seems much more complete and fulfilling than Arthur's. Lastly, Stan's mandalic vision in *The Tree of Man* is couched in writing of nervous excitement; there is a distinct effort on the novelist's part to invite his readers into sharing the character's experience; but in *The Solid Mandala* the vision has largely withdrawn into Arthur's incommunicativeness, since not even his sensuous dance of the mandala conveys the emotional fervour of the vision in the second last chapter of *The Tree of Man*.

I should like to argue, therefore, that by the time he wrote *The Solid Mandala* White seems to have become persuaded that only through absolute alienation from social existence can man have a possibility (no more than that) of visionary achievement; in *The Tree of Man*, however, Stan is able to triumph, as Bub Quigley cannot, because he has attempted to retain some connection with the ordinary aspects of consciousness. And this suggests that the unique historical concern of the novel is of great importance. Readers of the book must be puzzled why the author chose to contain his highly sophisticated preoccupations (even apart from his employment of Jungian material) in such an apparently naïve form as the pioneering novel. Clearly, his social attitudes, his pessimistic view of what becomes later on epitomized by Sarsaparilla, led him into the use of this form, but I think that it is equally connected with his preoccupation with visionary experiences. In the idyllic, in a sense prelapsarian world of the opening of the novel, where Stan and Amy, the man and the woman, live in close harmony with their environment, with the land and the animals which sustain them and which also depend on them, it was possible to achieve a richness of life without having to escape into the splendid but in a very real sense perverse world of the visionary. It seems to me that at the end of the novel Stan recaptures something that he had once possessed and which he must reconquer through his private world. Amy, his wife, also had a modicum of this integrity, but she is destroyed, as this antipodean Adam and Eve are cast out into the cruel world of the twentieth century, because she has not been able to achieve her husband's protective mandala. At the end of the novel she grows fat and suffers the Jungian affliction of inflation.

In this way, I would claim that White translates Jung's specifically clinical observations concerning the types of individuals who have mandalic experiences into terms of morality. Jung the scientist realized that extreme psychotic disorder frequently occasioned such experiences, and he found that encouragement of these visions, expressed in dreams, brought considerable relief and even ultimate cure to the patients. Jung the mystic then began to regard such experiences as the philosopher's stone which would cure the malaise of the twentieth century; the purely empirical connection between neurosis and mandalic experience became a panacea which would enable modern man to rise above the social and moral decadence of his century and to be reunited with his sense of the numinous—the basis of all religious experience without which man cannot exist. It is this that White seems to me to have adopted in his novels, and this is how these private eccentric experiences become parts of his larger concern with the human condition.

The Tree of Man, because it retains its contacts with a past, more fulfilling world, does not need to have its visionaries as extreme and as alienated as *The Solid Mandala*, which is placed so firmly in this century, needs to. But the last chapter of the novel gives us, nevertheless, a premonition of Arthur Brown in the Parkers' grandson, who wanders among the trees with *his* solid mandala, that piece of coloured glass his grandmother had given him, which had been left behind, many years ago, by the strange child the Parkers had rescued from the flood. And as the boy looks "through the glass at the crimson mystery of the world", he determines to write a poem, a poem of life, not of death as he thought earlier, a poem which would include everything, "urgent telegrams, and the pieces of torn letters that fall out of metal baskets". But in this, perhaps, he is to be frustrated, as Arthur Brown is frustrated, because despite the triumphant, hopeful ending to the novel—

> So that in the end there were the trees. The boy walking through them with his head drooping as he increased in stature. Putting out shoots of green thought. So that, in the end, there was no end.

—all he can do is "scribble on the already scribbled trees", and go back to the house where his grandfather died, to his grandmother's possessiveness, with a sense of his own greatness that is "still a secret". For this child, as for Arthur Brown, I suspect, the secret is always to remain—he has not had his grandfather's advantage; he lives in the modern world.   1/1967

A Reading of Patrick White's *Voss*

G. A. WILKES

Patrick White has himself traced the genesis of *Voss* to his experiences in the war, first in London and then in the Western Desert. "It was not until 1939," he has written, "after wandering by myself through most of Western Europe, and finally most of the United States, that I began to grow up and think my own thoughts."

The War did the rest. What had seemed a brilliant, intellectual, highly desirable existence, became distressingly parasitic and pointless. There is nothing like a rain of bombs to start one trying to assess one's own achievement. Sitting at night in his London bed-sitting room during the first months of the Blitz, this chromium-plated Australian with two fairly successful novels to his credit came to the conclusion that his achievement was practically nil. Perhaps significantly, he was reading at that time Eyre's *Journal*.[1]

The consequences of White's re-assessment of his achievement are to be seen in his two post-war novels, *The Aunt's Story* (1948) and *The Tree of Man* (1955). The third of them, *Voss* (1957), remains for him a book "possibly conceived during the early days of the Blitz, when I sat reading Eyre's *Journal* in a London bed-sitting room". The conception was then developed by his war experiences in the Middle East, and brought to maturity later:

Nourished by months spent trapesing backwards and forwards across the Egyptian and Cyrenaican deserts, influenced by the archmegalomaniac of the day, the idea finally matured after reading contemporary accounts of Leichhardt's expeditions and A. H. Chisholm's *Strange New World* on returning to Australia.

[1] Patrick White, "The Prodigal Son", *Australian Letters*, I (April 1958), 37-40. The two following quotations are also from this article.

It was in the desert, according to John Hetherington, that White first saw the novel as "built around a central character who was, like Hitler, a megalomaniac". This character was to be involved in "an unconsummated Tristan and Isolde love affair with a woman he was physically separated from"—a possibility "suggested to White by his work of censoring letters written by airmen to the wives and girls in England whom they were cut off from by the war".[2]

Although the relationship of *Voss* to the *Journals* of Eyre and Leichhardt—and especially to Chisholm's *Strange New World*, where Leichhardt is seen as blundering and psychopathic—repays investigation,[3] here I need only refer to the conception of "the explorer" offered in the novel itself. It is defined in a conversation between Colonel Hebden and Mrs de Courcy:

"Obsessed," she repeated, patting a bow of the dress which she could no longer feel suited her.
"I have lost the habit of civilised life," explained the Colonel . . . "If you had been a man, Effie, you might have become an explorer. You are sufficiently tenacious. Your thirst for conquest would have carried you over the worst of actual thirst."[4]

The explorer is one with a "thirst for conquest" which transcends "actual thirst": this is a motive ascribed to Voss from the outset, underlying the awkwardness of his behaviour in Sydney society in 1845, his clumsiness with the English language, his eccentric appearance. It sets him apart from the other members of the expedition, who come to regard him with either awe or fear. Voss expounds his purpose to Le Mesurier one evening in the Domain, urging the young man to accompany him:

"And your genius?" said the German.

[2] See John Hetherington, "Patrick White: Life at Castle Hill" in *Forty-Two Faces* (Cheshire, 1962). This "profile" seems to be partly based on conversations with White, who is quoted as saying "For some of that time in the desert I had a posting in which I was free to wander, and I covered a lot of ground. It was then that I began to realise the possibilities of the desert, and that the Voss character really had a chance to develop." (p. 144)
[3] See Marcel Aurousseau, "The Indentity of Voss", *Meanjin*, XXII (1958), 85-87; and J. F. Burrows, "*Voss* and the Explorers", *AUMLA* 26 (1966), 234-40.
[4] *Voss* (Eyre & Spottiswoode, 1957), p. 433. All page references are to this edition.

"What genius?" asked Le Mesurier, and let fall the last of his ammunition.

"That remains to be seen. Every man has a genius, though it is not always discoverable. Least of all when choked by the trivialities of daily existence. But in this disturbing country, so far as I have become acquainted with it already, it is possible more easily to discard the inessential and to attempt the infinite. You will be burnt up most likely, you will have the flesh torn from your bones, you will be tortured probably in many horrible and primitive ways, but you will realise that genius of which you sometimes suspect you are possessed, and of which you will not tell me you are afraid." (pp. 38-39)

Voss is a man obsessed, seeking in the inland an escape from "the trivialities of daily experience", using the expedition to mortify and exalt himself. He finds his selfhood in disdaining the ordinary values—disdaining the conventions and usages of the society in which he is placed, disdaining the natural beauty of the world for a private world of "desert and dreams", and disdaining the values that the mass of men revere. He seeks an ascendancy over all the members of his party, to prove to himself that their beliefs must surrender to his own—to his own illusion that man is immeasurable, that by throwing off debilitating notions of sympathy and humility, despising human weakness in himself and others, he may reach his full stature.

It is this effort to extinguish all human impulses in himself that makes Voss a tortured figure. At his first awkward encounter with Laura Trevelyan, when she receives him with biscuits and the second best port while the family is at church, Voss sees that she is beautiful, but

Such beautiful women were in no way necessary to him, he considered, watching her neck. He saw his own room, himself lying on the iron bed. Sometimes he would be visited by a sense of almost intolerable beauty, but never did such experience crystallise in objective visions. Nor did he regret it, as he lay beneath his pale eyelids, reserved for a peculiar destiny. He was sufficient in himself. (p. 17)

This passage catches at an element in the novel that is essential to its interpretation, and accounts for some of its most perplexing features. Voss on his "iron bed", lying "beneath his pale eyelids", is subject to visitations of "a sense of almost intolerable beauty". What is the beauty that threatens Voss's effort to be self-sufficient? It is hinted as, after his exhortation to Le Mesurier to realize his genius, the two walk back from the Domain towards the lights of the town. "The German began to think of the material world which his egoism had made him reject. In that world men and women sat at a round table and broke bread together. At times, he admitted, his hunger was almost unbearable" (p. 39). The material world which his egoism has renounced continues to haunt Voss, at times as a lighted window in the dusk, at times in the appeal of a Laura Trevelyan, but most often through the seductiveness of its own natural splendours—as he experiences them, for example, in the descent into the valley at Rhine Towers.

 Late in the afternoon of their arrival, the party descended from the hills into a river valley, of which the brown water ran with evening murmur and brown fish snoozed upon the stones. Now the horses pricked their ears and arched their necks tirelessly. They were all nervous veins as they stepped out along the pleasant valley. They were so certain. Which did, indeed, inspire even strangers with a certain confidence and sense of home-coming.
 Soon domestic cows had run to look, and horned rams, dragging their sex amongst the clover, were being brought to fold by a youthful shepherd. But it was the valley itself which drew Voss. Its mineral splendours were increased in that light. As bronze retreated, veins of silver loomed in the gullies, knobs of amethyst and sapphire glowed on the hills, until the horseman rounded that bastion which fortified from sight the ultimate stronghold of beauty.
 "*Achhh!*" cried Voss, upon seeing.
 Sanderson laughed almost sheepishly.
 "Those rocks, on that bit of a hill up there, are the 'Towers' from which the place takes its name."
 "It is quite correct," said the German. "It is a castle."
 This was for the moment pure gold. The purple stream of evening flowing at its base almost drowned Voss. Snatches of memory racing through him made it seem the more intolerable that he might not finally sink, but would rise as from other drownings on the same calamitous raft. (pp. 136-137)

Here the created world ("as bronze retreated, veins of silver loomed in the gullies, knobs of amethyst and sapphire glowed on the hills") is being rendered as on one of the occasions when its beauty proves intolerable and Voss, despite himself, is drowned by it. The consequences are felt as Mrs Sanderson comes out to join her husband in welcoming the party, and the grooms come to take the horses—while Voss remains in the saddle, "thoughtful, with his mouth folded in".

>The serpent has slid even into this paradise, Frank Le Mesurier realised, and sighed.
>Everyone was expecting something.
>"I did not think to impose upon you to this extent, Mr Sanderson," the German released his lip and replied. "It would embarrass me to think such a large party should inconvenience you by intruding under your roof-tree. I would prefer to camp down somewhere in the neighbourhood with my men, with our own blankets, beside a bivouac fire."
>Mrs Sanderson looked at her husband, who had turned rather pale.
>"It would not enter my head," said the latter.
>Since it had entered the German's, his eyes shone with bitter pleasure. Now the beauty of their approach to Rhine Towers appeared to have been a tragic one, of which the last fragments were crumbling in the dusk. He had been wrong to surrender to sensuous delights, and must now suffer accordingly. (p. 138)

The surrender to the beauty of Rhine Towers is something for which Voss must scourge himself, and the punishment—partly because it is an exertion of his will on others—becomes itself a source of "bitter pleasure". This world his ego has rejected solicits Voss not only through its natural splendours: it offers also human companionship that he must resist, ideals of conduct (in Palfreyman, for example) that seem to challenge his own, and even the devotion of a sheep-dog that may stir an impulse of affection in return. Voss is constantly racked by the compulsion to show himself immune to these dangers, and yet is constantly vulnerable to them. He realizes that Judd has detected his affection for the sheep-dog Gyp:

>"Gyp is in fine condition, sir," Judd remarked to Voss one day as they rode along.
>He knew the leader's fondness for the dog, and thought secretly to humour him in this way.
>The black bitch had, indeed, flourished since the sheep had

been abandoned and the ground had softened. She led a life of pleasure, and would trot back and forth on spongy feet, her long tongue lolling in pink health, her coat flashing with points of jet.

"She has never looked better," Judd ventured to add.

"Certainly," Voss replied.

He had ridden back for company, and now sensed that he had done wrong; he must suffer for it.

"Yes," he said, raising his voice. "She is eating her head off, and I have been considering for several days what must be done for the common good."

Both men were silent for a little, watching with cold fascination the activities of the fussy dog, who was passing and re-passing, and once laughed up at them.

"I have thought to destroy her," said the fascinated Voss, "since we have no longer sheep, hence, no longer any earthly use for Gyp."

Judd did not answer; but Harry Robarts, who was riding close by, at the heels of the cattle, looked up, and did protest:

"Ah, no sir! Kill Gyp?"

... Voss was grinning painfully.

"I would like very much to be in a position to enjoy the luxury of sentiment," he said.

Accordingly, when they made the midday halt, the German called to his dog, and she followed him a short way. When he had spoken a few words to her, and was looking into the eyes of love, he pulled the trigger. He was cold with sweat. He could have shot off his own jaw. Yet, he had done right, he convinced himself through his pain, and would do better to subject himself to further drastic discipline. (pp. 283-84)

In Voss's attempt to extinguish human sentiment, to murder the instinct of love in himself, one major trial is presented by Laura Trevelyan. Already in Sydney she had divined the secret purpose of the expedition, recognized that Voss was preparing himself for damnation, and her effort is to save Voss through love. His decision to delay at Jildra, missing the best of a good season, on the chance of receiving a letter from Laura, is a yielding to his human nature: it is followed by another of those passages in which the landscape appears in a startling light.

The simplicity of the clay-coloured landscape was very moving to the German. For a moment everything was distinct. In the foreground some dead trees, restored to life by the absence of hate, were glowing with flesh of rosy light. All life was dependent on the thin lips of light, compressed, yet breathing at the rim of the world.

"That will be convenient then, and I shall leave at once on the arrival of Thorndike."

Never had an issue of greater importance been decided so conclusively by an apparently insignificant event.

... So he explained, but did not tell, absorbed as he was in his discovery: that each visible object has been created for purposes of love, that the stones, even, are smoother for the dust. (pp. 191-92)

Here the material world is not merely revealed to Voss in its beauty ("some dead trees, restored to life by the absence of hate, were glowing with flesh of rosy light") but is seen also as transfigured: we are close to the experience of Stan Parker in *The Tree of Man*, who in his "illumination" in the storm also saw the world as irradiated, as if the darkness were daylight, "and he were in love with the heaving world, down to the last blade of wet grass".[5] So Voss at this moment is "absorbed ... in his discovery: that each visible object has been created for purposes of love, that the stones, even, are smoother for the dust."

The issues raised here are perhaps more worth inquiry than the supra-sensory communication of Voss and Laura that has so occupied the critics. Allowing for the degree that the "dreams" of Voss and Laura rely for their content (like the dreams of anyone else) on the memories each has of the other, there is little left in their experience which would exceed that of earlier White characters, such as Theodora Goodman or even Stan Parker. That only *Voss* should have prompted an outcry might suggest that in this novel White is being unwittingly inept in areas in which he had succeeded before—except that these apparently "untoward" effects do not seem unwitting, but the product of conscious design. White has not conceived *Voss* in entirely naturalistic terms:

Always something of a frustrated painter, and a composer *manqué*, I wanted to give my book the textures of music, the sensuousness of paint, to convey through the theme and characters of *Voss* what Delacroix and Blake might have seen, what Mahler and

[5] *The Tree of Man* (Eyre & Spottiswoode, 1956), p. 152.

Liszt might have heard. Above all I was determined to prove that the Australian novel is not necessarily the dreary, dun-coloured offspring of journalistic realism.[6]

Certainly what is conveyed in *Voss* exceeds what is transacted at the level of action and dialogue, and as the progress of the expedition is described—in passages of an almost hallucinatory quality—the novel projects an imaginative world in which the sayings and doings of the characters are only a subordinate part. In this world one may not dispute the *fact* of the parallel experiences of Laura in Sydney and Voss in the desert, sustained by a kind of clairvoyance, but may still find the management of them occasionally clumsy. The box of pears allowed to rot in the sickroom, so that Laura may share Voss's experience of putrescence, makes the parallel too forced—a symptom of the same over-insistent method that demands that the spiritual union of Voss and Laura must have a symbolic child in Rose Portion's daughter Mercy. When the action is accepted in non-naturalistic terms, this over-insistence is still apt to weaken the novel where it should be strong.

The critical flurry caused by the "telepathic" episodes, however, has obscured some more essential processes at work in the book, and has hindered inquiry into such questions as why the perception of a transfigured world ("dead trees . . . glowing with flesh of rosy light") should lead Voss to the discovery that "each visible object has been created for purposes of love". There is a disjunction between the perception and the discovery—or between the perception and the author's evaluation of it?—that one might expect the novel to explain. Laura, in one of her letters to Voss, describes a similar experience at the funeral of Rose Portion:

We buried her at the Sand Hills on an indescribable day, of heat, and cloud, and wind. As I stood there (I hesitate to write you all this, except that it is the truth), as I stood, the material part of myself became quite superfluous, while my understanding seemed to enter into wind, earth, the ocean beyond, even the soul of our poor, dead maid. I was nowhere and everywhere at once. I was destroyed, yet living more intensely that actual sunlight, so that I no longer feared the face of Death as I had found it on the

---

[6] "The Prodigal Son", *Australian Letters*, I (April 1958), 39.

pillow. If I suffered, it was to understand the devotion and suffering of Rose, to love whom had always been an effort! (p. 255)

This is a moment of the eclipse of the self, of its dissolution into wind, earth and the ocean beyond, through which it attains to a greater understanding and love. So much seems to be asserted: the assertion will not gather more meaning until Voss's history has been pressed further.

Although the contest of Voss with Laura is never relaxed, she is but one personality with whom he must grapple. Of the various members of his party, the simpleton Harry Robarts from the first accepts Voss as his prophet, and Turner and Angus are soon subjugated to him by their natural mediocrity: the challenge is to come from Judd, Palfreyman, and Le Mesurier. Outwardly the strongest nature, Judd proves eventually to have offered the least opposition. As an ex-convict who has felt the lash, Judd seems at first a man who has suffered his mortification in advance: he joins the expedition partly from a wish to serve, and partly in search of the fulfilment that he suspects may lie beyond the orbit of his present experience, like the worlds at the end of the telescope he has set up near his slab hut. Judd serves conscientiously, becoming almost the embodiment of the common-sense of the party. Eventually, however, his common-sense breaks down: forced to shoot a fallen and screaming horse, he then pelts it with stones (p. 359), and later, contemplating the remainder of their stock, decides to turn back:

The man-animal joined them [the horses and goats] and sat for a while upon the scorching bank. It was possibly this communion with the beasts that did finally rouse his bemused human intellect, for in their company he sensed the threat of the knife, never far distant from the animal throat.
"I will not! I will not!" he cried a last, shaking his emaciated body.
Since his own fat paddocks, not the deserts of mysticism, nor the transfiguration of Christ, are the fate of common man, he was yearning for the big breasts of his wife, that would smell of fresh-baked bread even after she had taken off her shift. (pp. 367-68)

Although the decision to return would seem a rational one, it is Judd "the man-animal" who makes it; the things that draw him back—his wife, his property, his son—are never to be regained, though he himself survives.

Le Mesurier, Voss's disciple, is to prove a more formidable adversary. He alone of the party understands the motives of the leader, and he alone experiences the beauty of Rhine Towers in a manner akin to Voss:

> Already the evening of his arrival, upon scenes of splendour such as he had known to exist but never met, Frank Le Mesurier had begun to change. The sun's sinking had dissolved all hardnesses. Darkness, however, had not fallen; it seemed, rather, to well forth, like the beating and throbbing of heart and pulse in the young man's body, to possess the expectant hills. Only the admirable house resisted. Later that night he had gone outside to watch the light from the lamps and candles, with which every window appeared to be filled. Isolation made that rather humble light both moving and desirable. So the days began to explain. Grasses were melting and murmuring. A child laid its cheek against him. The sun, magnificently imperious, was yet a simple circle that allowed him to enter, with the result that he was both blinded and illuminated. (p. 152)

Instead of resisting these experiences, and excoriating himself, Le Mesurier writes them down. They become the substance of the prose poems he enters in his journal as the expedition goes on—a habit that disturbs Voss, as evidence of some area of Le Mesurier's mind that is not subject to him. Le Mesurier comes to see it as his mission "to be present at the damnation of man, and to express faithfully all that I experience in my own mind" (p. 296). When Voss eventually gains possession of the notebook during Le Mesurier's illness, and reads the poems, they expose him to the force to which he had succumbed at Rhine Towers and at Jildra—invading his mind and wrestling with his will. His own aspiration is figured in these poems ("Man is King. They hung a robe upon him, of blue sky. His crown was molten. He rode across his kingdom of dust, which paid homage to him") but then juxtaposed with another reality:

> Humility is my brigalow, that must I remember: here I shall find a thin shade in which to sit. As I grow weaker, so I shall become strong. As I shrivel, I shall recall with amazement the visions of love, of trampling horses, of drowning candles, of hungry emeralds. Only goodness is fed.

Until the sun delivered me from my body, the wind fretted my wretched ribs, my skull was split open by the green lightning.

Now that I am nothing, I am, and love is the simplest of all tongues. (p. 316)

The recurring concept of the dissolution of the self in the created world ("the sun delivered me from my body, the wind fretted my wretched ribs") is associated in Le Mesurier's mind with aboriginal beliefs about the migration of spirits, which the party had encountered first in its discovery of the burial platform (pp. 260-62) and then in the ochre drawings in the cave. The drawings had reminded Voss how as a boy he had flown kites with messages attached to their tails, and "sometimes the string would break, and the released kite, if it did not disintegrate in the air, must have carried its message into far places; but, whatever the destination, he had never received a reply" (p. 293). Both destination and reply are hinted as Le Mesurier's poem takes up the motif of the ochre kangaroo:

Flesh is for hacking, after it has stood the test of time. The poor, frayed flesh. They chase this kangaroo, and when they have cut off his pride, and gnawed his charred bones, they honour him in ochre on a wall. Where is his spirit? They say: It has gone out, it has gone away, it is everywhere.

O God, my God, I pray that you will take my spirit out of this my body's remains, and after you have scattered it, grant that it shall be everywhere, and in the rocks, and in the empty waterholes, and in true love of all men, and in you, O God, at last.

When Voss had finished this poem, he clapped the book together.

"*Irrsinn!*" said his mouth.

He was protesting very gutturally, from the back of his throat, from the deepest part of him, from the beginning of his life.

If a sick man likes to occupy himself in this fashion, he decided.

But the sane man could not assert himself enough in the close cave.

He lay down again on his blanket, and was trembling. His mouth and throat were a funnel of dry leather.

I am exhausted, he explained, physically exhausted. That is all.

There remained his will, and that was a royal instrument.

(pp. 316-17)

Le Mesurier's prose-poems ask to be evaluated through their effect on Voss. They are the work of a man who has exposed himself to the reality of the material world that Voss's egoism has rejected, and who has been able to shed his sense of individuality in that exposure: a state in which he finds himself nearest to humility and love. Le Mesurier looks to the complete disintegration of the self in death, with his spirit then distributed everywhere, as the ultimate fulfilment—"after you have scattered it, grant that it shall be . . . in the rocks, and in the empty water-holes, and in true love of all men, and in you, O God, at last". Against this vision the tormented Voss sets his will, "and that was a royal instrument".

The only victory remaining to Voss's will, however, is the victory already mentioned over Judd, who is provoked to what Voss rejoices in as "disloyalty". This is preceded by what Voss at first senses to be a victory over Palfreyman, but finds eventually to have been his own undoing. Voss has tried persistently to betray Palfreyman into anger or chagrin, to expose his humility as something else masquerading as humility—much as he has tried to undermine Judd. He is rewarded by learning Palfreyman's secret: that he once failed his hunchback sister in love, and has joined the party seeking expiation and release ("he had failed her kisses, but would offer himself, as another sacrifice, to other spears"—p. 300). The theft by the natives of an axe, a bridle and a compass provides Voss with the opportunity to send Palfreyman among them unarmed, in the hope of "revealing the true condition of a soul". Palfreyman accepts the commission:

"No. I will go. I will trust to my faith."
It sounded terribly weak. Voss heard with joy, and looked secretly at the faces of the other men. These, however, were too thin to express anything positive.
Palfreyman, who was certainly very small, in what had once been his cabbage-tree hat, had begun to walk towards the cloudful of blacks, but slowly, but deliberately, with rather large strides, as if he had been confirming the length of an important plot of land . . . Over the dry earth he went, with his springy, exaggerated strides, and in this strange progress was at peace and in love with his fellows. Both sides were watching him. The aboriginals could have been trees, but the members of the expedition

were so contorted by apprehension, longing, love or disgust, they had become human again. All remembered the face of Christ that they had seen at some point in their lives, either in churches or visions, before retreating from what they had not understood, the paradox of man in Christ, and Christ in man. All were obsessed by what could be the last scene for some of them. They could not advance farther.

Voss was scourging his leg with a black stick.

Palfreyman walked on . . .

If his faith had been strong enough, he would have known what to do, but as he was frightened, and now could think of nothing, except, he could honestly say, that he did love all men, he showed the natives the palms of his hands. These, of course, would have been quite empty, but for the fate that was written on them. (pp. 364-65)

One black flings a spear, another stabs with a knife, and Palfreyman staggers to his knees:

The circles were whirling already, the white circles in the blue, quicker and quicker.

"Ah, Lord," he said, upon his knees, "if I had been stronger."

But his voice was bubbling. His blood was aching through a hole which the flies had scented already.

Ah, Lord, Lord, his mind repeated, before tremendous pressure from above compelled him to lay down the last of his weakness. He had failed evidently. (p. 365)

Has he failed? He has died, and died convinced of his weakness: but Voss has not been able to prove Palfreyman's faith an illusion. In his "strange progress" towards the blacks he has felt "at peace and in love with his fellows", so that those watching "all remembered the face of Christ that they had seen at some point in their lives", and in his weakness Palfreyman can finally think of nothing except that "he did love all men". Although he is in a sense a casualty of the faith he trusts in, the faith itself has endured the test.

Voss is to be insidiously conquered by it. Despising Palfreyman's ministrations to his suffering fellows ("Mr Palfreyman, in his capacity of Jesus Christ, lances the boils"—p. 259), Voss had nevertheless begun to vie with him, and had already found himself being taken charge of by the role he had assumed. As Palfreyman walks to his death, Voss is among the spectators constrained to remember "the face of Christ that they had seen at some point in their lives", and through the remainder of the narrative the influence of Palfreyman continues to be exerted on him. After the burial, "the Christ picture" returns to haunt Voss (p. 367); when he is later taken in charge by the blacks, then "because he was not accustomed to the gestures of humility, he tried to think how Palfreyman might have acted in similar circumstances" (p. 389); and when the whole expedition is seen in retrospect, Palfreyman and Voss have become indistinguishable in the memory of Judd, the only survivor.

So Voss's will, that "royal instrument", is broken. He confesses to Le Mesurier, "I have no plan, but will trust to God" (p. 403), and eventually calls to Christ: *"O Jesus, rette mich nur! Du lieber!"* (p. 415). Yet these last stages of Voss's history are not especially climatic. They are perhaps not intended to be, for in Voss's last dream of Laura they are seen as part of "the long journey back in search of human status" (p. 418). We are to see Voss becoming human again, acquiring the inadequacies that "human status" implies. Voss's attainment of humility is nevertheless not so compelling dramatically as his resistance of it had been, and the earlier tortured Voss, trying to annihilate human feeling in himself, remains the dominating figure. When therefore Laura Trevelyan, in an interval in her fever, announces that "When man is truly humbled, when he has learnt that he is not God, then he is nearest to becoming so. In the end, he may ascend" (p. 411), this is something that the novel has hardly demonstrated.

The statement is, however, Laura's, and the point may be that Voss's history has demonstrated it to her. The critical tendency to find some religious message in the utterances of the characters towards the end of *Voss* should be resisted. Certainly White himself has declared that "the state of simplicity and humility is the only desirable one for artist or man. While to reach it may be impossible, to attempt to do so is imperative".[7] Yet the only explicitly religious concepts found in *Voss* are those appropriate to the characters. Voss's drama is worked out as an attempt to rival Christ, to undergo the same sufferings in order to deify himself, to prove that man can become

---

[7] "The Prodigal Son", *Australian Letters*, I (April 1958), 39.

God: the terms of the conflict, the insight of Laura into it, and its outcome, are all part of the framework of beliefs of the participants (in literary terms, this is the "myth" of which the novel avails itself). Palfreyman's beliefs are likewise his own, and they are sometimes viewed ironically, as before the magnificence of Rhine Towers. "Even Palfreyman realised he had failed that day to pray to God, and must forfeit what progress he had made on the road where progress is perhaps illusory" (p. 137). When Laura Trevelyan's statements about God lead Dr Kilwinning to think that other help than his own is needed, she replies laughing: "Dear Aunt," she said, "you were always bringing me soups, and now it is a clergyman" (p. 412).

Voss's "conversion" is a conversion in terms of his own thinking, but this is not the only evaluation of it that the novel gives. The novel offers, for example, an independent "mythical" structure in the aboriginal beliefs about the migration of souls, and the distribution of the spirit through nature after death. Harry Robarts interprets the death of Palfreyman in these terms when he sees the white bird departing from his side (p. 366); the rock drawings influence Voss, recalling the kites he had released in the air, carrying their messages to far places; Le Mesurier embodies these conceptions in his prose-poems, and is able to answer Harry's questions about death:

> "Dying is creation. The body creates fresh forms, the soul inspires by its manner of leaving the body, and passes into other souls."
> "Even the souls of the damned?" asked Voss. (p. 385)

Even the souls of the damned. The most inclusive scheme of ideas in the book—the aboriginal beliefs may be seen as an aspect of it—is the scheme in which Voss is in a contest with the "intolerable beauty" of the natural world, losing his selfhood in surrender to it. Le Mesurier undergoes the same experience at Rhine Towers, and even more dramatically in his ride through the storm (p. 266); Laura, too, at the funeral of Rose Portion, had felt the material part of herself become quite superfluous, as her understanding entered into wind, earth and the ocean beyond (p. 255). I find some difficulty in the imaginative leap that is made from this dissolution of the ego to the state of humility and love: it is not that the two states are unrelated, but that there is a shift from the presentation of an experience (which, although esoteric, can be followed through) to the fixing of a value upon it in more conceptual terms. It is in the main, however, the value fixed by the characters. It is for Laura that her experience at the funeral seems to bring an access of understanding; it is to Voss at Jildra that the "dead trees . . . glowing with flesh of rosy light" bring an awakening that "each visible object has been created for purposes of love"; it is in Le Mesurier that the shedding of his human personality creates the awareness that "Humility is my brigalow, that must I remember". This framework in the novel comes to subsume the aboriginal motif, and extends beyond the drama of salvation.

Voss's story is not complete when the decision to "trust in God" rescues him from the damnation he has been courting. There are still three intriguing chapters through which his history is being appraised. Although these chapters describe incidentally the final expiry of the expedition, with the deaths of Turner and Angus, then of Dugald and Jackie, and the ineffective forays of Colonel Hebden, their main effect is to return the narrative to the milieu of social gatherings in Sydney, and to view it with a greater detachment. The final chapter is concerned with the unveiling, twenty years afterwards, of a bronze statue of Voss in the Domain, at a ceremony attended by Laura, Colonel Hebden, old Sanderson—and Judd. Cared for in the wilderness by the blacks, Judd is restored to civilization with his mind wandering, his possessions gone—the fate of the man "wedded to earthly things", whose soul "had achieved fulfilment not by escaping from his body, but by returning to it" (p. 261). He describes to Laura the contrary fate of Voss: "The blacks talk about him to this day. He is still there—that is the honest opinion of many of them—he is there in the country, and always will be" (p. 472). The last word is spoken by Laura to the English visitor Ludlow, who interrogates her about "this familiar spirit, whose name is upon everybody's lips, the German fellow who died".

"Voss did not die," Miss Trevelyan replied. "He is there still, it is said, in the country, and always will be. His legend will be written down, eventually, by those who have been troubled by it."

"Come, come. If we are not certain of the facts, how is it possible to give the answers?"

"The air will tell us," Miss Trevelyan said.

By which time she had grown hoarse, and fell to wondering aloud whether she had brought her lozenges. (pp. 477-78)

This is our final image of Voss, one from which the values of "humility" and "love" have somewhat receded. I do not suggest that the significance of the novel is to be found in the conclusion—the "significance" is co-extensive with the novel—but the conclusion is to be reckoned with. *The Aunt's Story* had traced the progress of Theodora Goodman towards "that desirable state . . . which resembles, one would imagine, nothing more than air or water";[8] and *The Tree of Man* had shown Stan Parker, in his successive "illuminations", achieving a state of oneness with the created world—a state which was nevertheless the measure of his apartness from that world's inhabitants, so that fulfilment for Stan (as for Theodora, despite the claims of Holstius) comes through transcendence. The way of transcendence is what is explored in *Voss*. Voss seeks it through the exaltation of his ego, which is humbled and brought to nothing. Yet he does achieve transcendence of a kind, in a manner he had not sought; his spirit is dispersed in the country, and his legend persists for those who have been troubled by it. The claim being made is the reverse of extravagant. The last chapter presents quite realistically the inheritors of the legend: the society he had left behind, represented in the "substantial citizens" at the unveiling of the statue, for whom Voss is "hung with garlands of rarest newspaper prose" (p. 468), and in the typical English visitor, Ludlow—and also in Laura Trevelyan, Colonel Hebden, and Judd. Although these last are set apart, they are still individually confused, and unable to communicate with one another. The astringent realism of this situation puts Voss's achievement in an ironical perspective, even as it lends credence to Le Mesurier's statement:

"Dying is creation. The body creates fresh forms, the soul inspires by its manner of leaving the body, and passes into other souls." (p. 385)

[8] *The Aunt's Story* (Routledge & Kegan Paul, 1948), p. 151.

Voss survives only in those few who have been "troubled" by his legend, as in *The Solid Mandala* Arthur Brown, after he has been taken to the asylum, will survive through Mrs Poulter. This may be little enough. But for each of them (as for her) the whole *Zeitgeist* has been changed by the experience.

3/1967

III PLAYS AND SHORT STORIES

Maenads and Goat-Song: The Plays of Patrick White

THELMA HERRING

Before trying to distinguish what is individual in a writer's work it is helpful to set him in a literary context; but to what should we relate the plays of Patrick White?[1] Certainly not to any local tradition, since (Douglas Stewart's verse plays being *sui generis*) the work of no other Australian dramatist exists in the same dimension. Nor can he be usefully related to the contemporary drama of England, the spiritual bankruptcy of which is reflected in the inflated reputation of Harold Pinter, to whom many critics devote the same reverent attention as they more deservedly give to Beckett. Naturally, then, one turns to the Americans. Albee? At first sight very different; but a comparison suggests itself between *Who's Afraid of Virginia Woolf?* with its Strindbergian theme of the conflict between an unsuccessful academic and his dominating wife and *Night on Bald Mountain* with its Ibsenite theme of the conflict between an academic who is a failure as a human being and the wife whom he dominates (one recognizes an analogy between Sword and Miriam and such characters as Rosmer and Beata, Solness and Aline). And behind Albee there is the figure of O'Neill, a tireless experimenter like White, to whom he is inferior in mastery of language, in subtlety, in comic sense, but a brilliantly inventive dramatist and a writer as eager as White himself to "possess the infinite" and never afraid to take tremendous risks in the attempt: there is internal evidence to suggest that White has studied O'Neill's work to good purpose, and *Night on Bald Mountain* could also be des-

[1] *Four Plays* (Eyre and Spottiswoode, 1965). All page-references are to this edition.

cribed as literally and metaphorically a long day's journey into night. Of White, as of O'Neill, one can say that he is firmly in the great central tradition of modern drama deriving from the two Scandinavian masters, Ibsen and Strindberg. I shall indicate other possible influences and affinities at specific points.

Having acknowledged their place in a tradition one needs to add that White's plays, like his novels, are in their ultimate effect completely individual, the products of a sustained poetic vision of life and an extraordinary command of the resources of language. They share this integrity of vision and style, yet they differ strikingly from each other: neither as dramatist nor as novelist is White content to repeat himself, despite the recurrence of certain symbols, the reworking of themes. His novels tempt one to think of him as a Himalayan mountaineer, surrounded by peaks which he has to attempt because they are there: but the artist, of course, is of necessity a Hermann Buhl, unorthodox among climbers, in that he makes his death-or-glory ascent alone and unsupported. Sometimes, as in *Voss*, it is dizzying to watch the struggle, and one wonders whether White himself is ever dizzied or simply exhilarated as he conquers the awe-inspiring obstacles to his ascent. When *Riders in the Chariot* appeared the puzzling question arose in one's mind where he *could* go from there: his forthcoming novel will of course supply the answer, but in the meantime no one who cares about the survival of the theatre could fail to be interested in his turning again to drama, the form which first attracted him. It would be foolish to look for a *Voss* in this first volume of plays; but what seems to me truly exciting is the evidence it offers of the right equipment to meet the challenge, of initiative and stamina and an intellectual grasp of the problems to be solved.

It is significant that the four plays are of increasing complexity and that each offers a different kind of answer to the modern prose dramatist's problem of finding a method that escapes the jejune flatness of pure naturalism on the one hand and the inhuman schematism of pure expressionism on the other. The first, *The Ham Funeral*, written as long ago as 1947, and shorter than the others, is a symbolic play; it has a setting which suggests London but from the beginning it avoids localization, just as the generic labels of the dramatis personae, together with the allegorically suggestive names given to the Landlord and his wife, Will and Alma Lusty, point to an avoidance of the particular in characterization. *The Season at Sarsaparilla* employs a large cast and works through a group technique, interweaving the affairs of three adjoining households: expressionistic devices such as the razzle-dazzle of time and motion on which the characters perform like automata, invisible props and mime are used intermittently. *A Cheery Soul*, the boldest experiment of all, has a naturalistic first act, then switches abruptly to expressionism in the second act, with its chorus of old women and its flash-backs into the life of Mrs Lillie and her dead husband; the third act opens with a choral ode by the old women ironically celebrating the coming of spring, and in the impressive church scene passes beyond external reality as the light deepens into the "glow of inwardness" and the characters articulate the "litany of their personal hopes and fears". The nearest parallel, technically, which occurs to me is in *The Silver Tassie*, the second act of which, culminating in the satirical litany to the gun, provides a similar jolting contrast in method to the first; but whereas O'Casey returns to his original group of characters in later acts, the Custances who share the foreground with Miss Docker in the first act of *A Cheery Soul* make only a fleeting appearance thereafter—which imposes on the audience a pretty difficult task of re-orientation. *Night on Bald Mountain*[2] is a primarily naturalistic play with submerged symbolism, in the manner of late Ibsen: it is constructed with a virtuosity that Ibsen might have admired, and a symmetry that is itself of symbolic significance. Opening at dawn outside Miss Quodling's shack on Bald Mountain, with a monologue addressed by Miss Quodling to her goats, it follows this with another short scene in the bush before moving in I, iii to the interior of the Swords' house, where it remains for the unbroken second act: Act III contains three scenes which reverse

[2] The splendidly atmospheric title recalls that of Moussorgsky's well-known orchestral fantasia, based on the Witches' Sabbath incident in Gogol's "St. John's Eve". Though Gogol's story has no connection with White's play, by its use of the devil and witchcraft it has an associative link with the *Walpurgisnacht* after which Act II of *Who's Afraid of Virginia Woolf?* is named. Is it also relevant to point out that there are hints of the Faust-Gretchen myth in the story of Sword and Stella?

the movement of Act I, ending at dawn twenty-four hours later with another monologue by Miss Quodling. Thus the outer scenes provide a framework of nature, the mountain and the animal world, to give perspective to the main scenes in which the action moves inwards, peeling away the layers of pretence till the souls of Hugo and Miriam Sword are laid bare: a stripping process less jaggedly and brutally horrifying but ultimately just as unsparingly revealing as that in Albee's play. Here and in his first two plays, White makes ingenious use of a multiple set: in *The Ham Funeral* the contrast between the basement, where the Young Man encounters the crude realities of life and death, and the ground floor of the "great, damp, crumbling house" where he meditates and converses with his insubstantial anima is part of the play's basic symbolism; in *The Season at Sarsaparilla* the simultaneous view of the three "brick boxes" in Mildred Street facilitates the presentation of the cycle of suburban life, punctuated by such rituals as the consumption of eggs; in *Night on Bald Mountain* the simultaneous showing of different rooms of the house (a device which O'Neill used very skilfully in *Desire Under the Elms*, but on a smaller scale) is an aid to the deeper probing into the characters' tangled and tortured relationships.

The problem of language, however, is the crucial one, and it is here that White can make his most valuable contribution. Anyone who has chewed over the indigestible dialogue of many modern naturalistic plays must welcome the opportunity of savouring a play written in his rich and piquant prose: that so intelligent a writer should even temporarily renounce the freer conventions of the novel and submit to the exacting discipline of writing imaginative dialogue that will be viable in the theatre is something to be profoundly grateful for.

From the beginning, in the Young Man's opening address to the audience in *The Ham Funeral*, he displays an easy mastery of non-naturalistic speech. Here, of course, his task is partly simplified by the fact that his protagonist is an aspiring poet whose senses are abnormally alert and who can talk naturally in metaphors, of life as a "mad, muddy mess of eels", of "the voices of the gas-fires", and so on; what is more remarkable is the way in which he modulates into a poetic use of the vernacular in the Landlady's speech, as in her soliloquy in I, ii:

This part of the 'ouse 'as never been warmed. I bet not even a first-class weddin' could chafe life into the stairs. Nor all the rice an' rudery in the world . . . The mice squeak behind the skirtin'-boards. Look 'ow the damp's spread. You could teach geography off the wall. (*Pausing as she mounts, tracing an outline with her finger*) 'Ole continents to them that knows. Africa couldn't be darker to me . . . (pp. 19-20).

So, too, in *Night on Bald Mountain*, the educated speech of Professor Sword can unobtrusively lift the dialogue to another plane:

Ever since we came to live in this house, we've been filling it with talk! (*Removed temporarily from his surroundings*) The mists have more to show for their activities . . . Down in the gully the sassafras grows green, the ferns never want for moisture, the rotting leaves create . . . silence. (p. 324)

But the most distinctive achievement, linguistically, is the earthy exuberant idiom of Miss Quodling. Her opening aria is an astonishing virtuoso performance; the unmistakable voice ranges from the colloquial humour of her invective:

Dolores! You leave Jessica alone! (*Sound of blows, bells and commotion*) If there's anything I hate, it's a goat with horns. You're a cow of a goat at times. Think you can run the yard. Wall-eyed, cow-hocked thing! I *hate* you, bloody Dolores! (*Pause. Silence*) (*Softly, tenderly*) No, I don't. Dolores? You're the best. The best! Eh? My Dolores! (*Genuinely remorseful and enraptured*) You've got the face of a regular Christian. (p. 270)

to the vivid imagery of her meditative hymn to the risen sun:

Mornun' . . . I love it even when it skins yer! Oh, yes, it can hurt! . . . When the ice crackles underfoot . . . and the scrub tears the scabs off yer knuckles . . . and the spiders' webs are spun again . . . first of all . . . out of dew . . . it's to remind that life begins at dawn. Bald Mountain! I wasn't born here. Oh, no! But know it, how I know it! I've learnt to understand the silences of rocks. Only the barren can understand the barren . . . (p. 272)

Is there another modern prose play which opens so magnificently as this? And although Miss Quodling's goats, as we come to see, have their relevance to the theme of the play, in a historical sense too what more appropriate beginning for a tragedy could be found than a goat-song?

White's wonderfully accurate ear has been widely praised (it is so impressive, indeed, that one hardly dares to suggest that just once or twice there is perhaps a minute lapse into an idiom that is specifically English rather than Australian): but such accuracy, though an invaluable asset, as absolute pitch is to a musician, is not in itself enough: it is the superb selection and organization which make even basically naturalistic dialogue dramatic and give it an individual tone. This can be seen in the dialogue of *The Season at Sarsaparilla*, which, although much closer to ordinary speech than that of *The Ham Funeral*, gains heightened significance from its context: like Chekhov, White not only interweaves different threads of action but counterpoints various conversational themes in a kind of fugue so that one can be an implicit comment on another. So, too, in a darker mood, there is the juxtaposition of Sword's comments on his wife to Denis Craig and Miriam's bitter speculations to Stella on her husband's probable disclosures about her to their guest in the first act of *Night on Bald Mountain* (pp. 294-95).

As compared with the even tone of the dialogue of a naturalistic play, White's language has rather the freedom and variety of an operatic score (one is reminded of Granville-Barker's instructions to his actors to treat a Shaw play like an Italian opera, and Shaw's own description of his dialogue in musical terms). He uses many kinds of formal and stylized speech: not only the long-established non-naturalistic conventions of soliloquy and choric speech and direct address to the audience (as when Miss Docker harangues them on Tom Lillie's death, p. 222) but more sophisticated experiments, many of them developed from the *Strange Interlude* technique, such as "double soliloquy" (pp. 98, 155), the stylized utterance of a thought sequence by the members of the Pogson family (p. 136), the parallel reveries of Miriam and Miss Quodling as they drink together (pp. 312 ff.), the passages of "recitative" in *The Ham Funeral*. There is even a faint reminiscence of the style of the plays of Auden and Isherwood in the satirical rhetoric of the Chorus in Act II of *A Cheery Soul*:

Was it necessary? Was it kind? ... At least she has her pension. She has her health. She has her cup of Ovaltine at bedtime. She has her awfully cheery nature—her goodness which can only be escaped by car ... She knows what is good for *you*. She knows what is *good*. Then what is wrong? or bad? (*Suddenly oracular*) Ask the piebald cat! (pp. 230-31).

One may have one's doubts about the extreme variations in style in *A Cheery Soul*, but in part of that play, in *The Ham Funeral*, in parts of *Night on Bald Mountain*, White has demonstrated that a more richly imaginative speech is attainable in prose drama that Eliot, approaching the problem of contemporary stage dialogue through the medium of verse, was able to achieve after he misguidedly denied himself free use of the imagery which gave poetic distinction to *The Family Reunion*.

The Ham Funeral, the only one of these plays that I have been fortunate enough to see on the stage, is a study of a young man's discovery of himself and of life, and the problem, as the author pointed out in his programme note, was "how to project a highly introspective character on the stage without impeding dramatic progress". In order to externalize the self-searchings of his protagonist, who is presented as an engaging mixture of diffidence and secret self-assurance, he uses the Girl whom he describes in Jungian fashion as the Young Man's anima, the voice of his "other self", while the Landlord and the Landlady, "the figures in the basement ... passion and compassion locked together" (pp. 69-70), are contrasting aspects of the reality with which the idealistic young man must wrestle. The Landlady, rapacious for "life" as symbolized by the whelks and the flares, lives through her senses and therefore in the present moment: the Landlord, immobile in his woollen underclothes, has intuitions of a spiritual reality and the deceptiveness of the senses:

I sit 'ere. I am content. Life, at last, is wherever a man 'appens to be. This 'ouse is life. I watch it fill with light, an' darken. These are my days and nights. The solid 'ouse spreadin' above my head. Only once in a while I remember the naked bodies ... knotting together ... killing theirselves ... and one another ... Bloody deluded! (p. 27)

To him "This table is love ... if you can get to know it" (p. 27), as potato peelings are oracles to the Girl (p. 32) and a vision of crimson rhubarb, according to Mr Wakeman in *A Cheery Soul*, "more articulate in praise than the chaos of a dark mind" (p. 247). The insistence on the illumination which may be attained through inanimate or natural objects is of course familiar to readers of White's novels.

Like Lear, the Young Man asks the question: "Who am I?" (p. 43)—uncertain whether he is a poet who will "possess the infinite" or "just an ineffectual prig" (p. 68); the play does not attempt any Shakespearean profundities in probing it, but it does present the Young Man's gropings in a mood of troubled urgency. The Landlady cannot answer—to her he is alternatively her lover and her dead child, and she forces him to slip in and out of their identities; the Landlord, although "he glimmered for a moment, and I almost saw his soul" (p. 41), dies before he can question him. But through a series of experiences, the quarrel between the Lustys which reveals that the Landlord is still subject to human passions, the Landlord's death, the grotesque wake at which he encounters the Relatives, expressionistically presented figures whom the programme note describes as "an expression of the conscience, with its multiple forebodings", and his subsequent seduction by Mrs Lusty, the Young Man is forced to confront reality.

Within its chosen limits the play seems to me almost completely successful. The action may be slight, but the range of tone is considerable, from the dream-like delicacy of the scenes with the Girl to the vigorous realism of the Lustys' quarrel, from the hilarious humour of the scavenging ladies to the stylized, sardonic, slightly sinister comedy of the Relatives. I would make only two criticisms. The first is that after witnessing two performances and reading it a number of times, I remain unpersuaded that the rending of its texture in the farcical interlude of the two scavengers, those less malevolent forerunners of Mrs Jolley and Mrs Flack, serves a useful purpose. Not that the interlude is without its thematic point: the discovery of the dead foetus, like the suicide of the pregnant Julia in *The Season at Sarsaparilla*, contributes to the cycle of "birth, copulation, and death", but the allusions to the Landlady's dead child have already supplied this motif.

At worst, however, it is a minor and local blemish. My second objection is much harder to formulate: it relates to something more pervasive and much more fundamental but also much less tangible which didn't in fact trouble me in the theatre: but because it applies also to some of White's later work I mention it at the risk of distorting my response to *The Ham Funeral* itself. Briefly, it is a slight feeling of dissatisfaction with the status accorded to Mrs Lusty in the scheme of the play. Not the least of D. H. Lawrence's disservices to English literature was his persuading a number of good writers, even one of the stature of Patrick White, that they have a moral duty to make genuflexions towards Life, conceived in Lawrentian terms: and the pity of it in White's case, as I see it, is that although of course one cannot doubt the sincerity of these large affirmations, they occur in parts of his work where he sometimes seems to be writing against the grain: whereas at his finest he communicates a different (not necessarily contradictory) wisdom. If Mrs Lusty, slobbering among her cockroaches, represents the Life the Young Man is required to accept, what, one wants to protest, is there to revere, why should anyone want it on these terms? Lawrence himself in his saner moments knew that it is the *quality of lives* that counts: who has shown this truth better than the author of *The Aunt's Story* and *Voss*? At a purely symbolic level one cannot impeach the moral that the Young Man must come to terms with the flesh; but at a symbolic level one would expect the flesh to be made a little more alluring. Mrs Lusty, however, unlike the Relatives, is not purely symbolic: she comes to life on the stage as a person, which is all to the good dramatically, but in doing so she raises questions about the theme. It is not that White is offering her as a solution: the Young Man leaves her in the end and goes off like Marchbanks into the night, knowing, like the Landlord, that "flesh . . . isn't the final answer", that warmth is *not* everything: it is the Landlord's belief that a human being must purge himself of his own evil that should emerge as the deepest truth—but perhaps it doesn't emerge quite strongly enough simply because the Landlady is such an overwhelming figure in the latter part of the play and because such a line as the Girl's "those who live also create" (p. 69) does seem to give a spurious validity to her "quality" of life.

Alma Lusty is the first of a series of women embodying Dionysiac values, whom for convenience we may describe as maenads. Miriam Sword is a tragic maenad destroyed by the Gothic (White's epithet—O'Neill would have said Christian) asceticism of her husband. In a dissimilar sense one might even see a very different character, Miss Docker, whom the Life Force certainly impels, as a maenad destroying that hapless Orpheus the Reverend Gregory Wakeman (after all, in Christian allegory Orpheus became a type of the crucified Christ, and hence of the good priest). Here, the maenad is a target for devastating satire; but in Nola Boyle we have a maenad who, like Mrs Lusty, is presented with a good deal of sympathy. Perhaps relatively more than she deserves? Nola's excuse is that "she wasn't born mean" (p. 98) (a point of view that leads to the apotheosis of Daise Morrow in "Down at the Dump"): "I bet some women aren't all that good. They just haven't got the kind of glands it takes to make a person go to the pack" (p. 150). But this is a dangerous argument that cuts both ways: for if it's all a matter of glands, the Girlie Pogsons are just as entitled to sympathy as the Nolas, and could fairly plead, inverting Lawrence's inelegant phrase, that "life has done dirt on" them, depriving them, to say the least, of a lot of pleasure; and the appropriate comment would seem to be Anna Christie's: "We're all poor nuts, and things happen, and we yust get mixed in wrong, that's all." The argument is, of course, Nola's, not the dramatist's: but the presentation can hardly be said to be impartial. (Maenads are even entitled to their Mixmasters and Wilton squares, it seems—whereas there is no mercy for Girlie's preoccupation with clean lino!)

That said, it must be admitted that some of the most amusing satire in *The Season at Sarsaparilla* is directed at Girlie's reminiscences of her girlhood on that "lovely property" Rosedale among the "hand-picked country stock" and that the finest scenes are undoubtedly the postlapsarian ones of recrimination and reconciliation between Nola and her two men, in which the taut dialogue expresses far more by what it omits than by what it states and the charting of the characters' fluctuating emotions is unerringly accurate. No play containing such scenes could be negligible: but it is not finally an advantage that the method of presentation requires a balance of attention to the affairs of the three households. We see too much of the Knotts and the elder Pogsons—though it is tantalizing not to see more of Roy and Judy. The latter is a delicate sketch of "the girl next door", sweet without insipidity: as for Roy Child, I cannot understand the general condemnation—it is surely desirable to have one character possessing some awareness among so many who are deficient in that quality. Despite these and other felicities such as the adroit use (especially at the end of the first act) of the child Pippy as an observer linking the human and animal worlds and the brilliant "placing" of mateship, R.S.L. version (the sentimental appearance and the often brutal reality), *The Season at Sarsaparilla* with its treatment of the theme of eternal recurrence seems to me inherently the least interesting of the four plays. Suburbia is hell on earth, to be sure, to those capable of bursting out "in a shower of glorious fireworks" (p. 90), and pregnant women do give birth sooner or later, and bitches, we know, will be bitches, even if they are human and have kind hearts —but White can show us more illuminating truths than these, and does so in his next two plays.

The second Sarsaparillan play, *A Cheery Soul*, is adapted from what I consider to be White's best short story—and it is remarkable how little adaptation is needed in the first act. One's immediate judgment is likely to be that he has made his point supremely well in the story and that it stands to lose more than it gains by transference to the stage. Miss Docker, that embodiment of the sin of militant virtue, is a character of wonderful vitality and freshness, but we get to know her through her encounters with a series of minor figures, and as the play alters focus one is conscious of a lack of dramatic impetus and the loss of the author's ironic comments. The mixture of modes does not work well, so far as I can judge in reading: Act II especially is a problem, and the more straightforward narrative version is much to be preferred. Again, though one notes the ingenuity with which Mr Wakeman's soliloquy (p. 247) is developed from two passages of narrative (*The Burnt Ones* pp. 180, 182), it is open to the objection that the eloquence of the authorial voice comes oddly even in soliloquy from a man cursed by inarticulateness. To leap to the conclusion that the story is superior at all points, however, would be a radical error: for the third act of *A Cheery Soul* surpasses all White's previous work in drama and is even better than the original narrative, in its fleshing out of the characters of the Wakemans, the elaboration of the church scene, and the addition to the final scene of Miss Docker's encounter with the swaggie.

The Wakemans suffer, like so many of White's characters, from the difficulty of communication, but in other respects, they are almost unique in that they are Christians with the goodness of *real* humility, a husband and wife whose marriage attains a happiness of a finer kind than the insulated connubial bliss of the Custances. In particular, Mary Wakeman (Alice in the story—for some reason she is renamed but declares that Mary isn't her real name; surely an audience would be puzzled?) is a remarkable miniature portrait of a young woman who is a refreshing contrast to the maenads. Awkward, inarticulate, a little priggish, capable of physical passion but not at the mercy of her glands, she is one of the very few women in White's work since Alys Browne of *Happy Valley* of whom it could be said that she knows the meaning of love, as her prayer in the litany proves:

> Give him, dear Lord, not the strength of lions, but that of ordinary, callous men. Break me, Lord, if You will, but leave him straight and beautiful. (p. 254)

The necessary expansion of the scene in All Saints is a brilliant piece of writing. If one regrets the loss of the description of Miss Docker singing, "her leathery soprano lashing the architraves", the experience of hearing the hymn itself would be ample compensation: and the litany gives scope for some incisive satire, such as the juxtaposition of Mr Wakeman's "If I am shortly to be judged, O Lord . . . ", and Miss Docker's "If I am about to judge, O Lord . . . ", and the supplications of the voices of suburbia:

> O Lord, the Egg Board . . .
> O Lord of justice, Woolworths and the supermarkets are driving us out!

Dear Lord, we cannot talk like our daughters-in-law. Do not let them laugh at us. (p. 255)

With the horrifying death of Mr Wakeman—a symbolic murder—there enters the play a darker, more passionate vein of feeling which is to dominate *Night on Bald Mountain*. It exposes the dangerous and sinister potentialities in Miss Docker's militant virtue: at the same time it is greatly to the dramatist's credit that he does not present her as the completely evil figure suggested by Mrs Wakeman's rather melodramatic accusation. Even Miss Docker's insensibility can be penetrated occasionally, as when after telling Mr Wakeman "the truth" about his sermons she "catches a glimpse of something which begins to cause her pain" (p. 246) and when "most unhappy, thoughtful" she is hurt by the implications of the children's tactless talk (p. 251). These are additions in the play, and the stage-directions make their purport plain. The final humanizing change is at the end, after the degradation of the cattle-dog's "judgment" on her, when the swaggie asks her for help and Miss Docker responds—angrily, but she does respond: "Here's a shilling. I'm poor, you know." It is a superb touch: as she goes off, shattered but still struggling to put on a bold front, we can deny her neither pity nor a measure of reluctant admiration. It is not the elements in White's work that happen to be fashionable, but those that are splendidly individual, that constitute his greatness: the vision that can embrace simultaneously both the tragedy of the Wakemans and the tragedy of Miss Docker is as rare as it is wonderful.

Night on Bald Mountain, though a flawed play and not the masterpiece it would have been if it had remained on the level of its opening, is much the finest in the volume. With a small cast of intelligent and articulate characters, using Ibsen's retrospective technique to probe the past conflicts that have produced the present state of anguished division, White is able to explore the situation in depth. Hugo Sword (both names are symbolic) is a Professor of English whose intellect and religious faith are alike sterile and destructive: his wife Miriam, having had her love and her artistic impulses stifled by him, has become a dipsomaniac and is masochistically engaged in self-destruction. I have already suggested a possible comparison with *Who's Afraid of Virginia Woolf?* At first the comparison between the two warring couples is decidedly in Albee's favour: the Swords are more conventionally conceived and do not make such a startling impact as George and Martha (though I may be *partly* influenced in this opinion by the advantage of having seen the dazzling New York production of Albee's play). It is not perhaps really important that George and Martha seem to belong more to their environment: Sword strikes one as a Casaubon of the Oxbridge donneries of an earlier period, an inhabitant of a more dignified world than that in which Chairs proliferate like chain-stores and their occupants are too busy attending committee meetings or projecting their personalities on TV to pore over literary effusions of their own in the privacy of their studies. What *is* troubling is a sense of predetermined attitudes, a weighting of sympathy in favour of the maenad (of whose "daemon", which has to be taken on trust, one may remain sceptical) and a suspicion that Sword is being hounded by his creator. This suspicion diminishes, however, as the play progresses. As Sword is stripped of his protective covering he becomes more human and in the third act his struggles to bridge the gap which he has seen at the end of Act II: "We'll never get through . . . never . . . never . . . however long we live . . . however many messages we send . . ." (p. 327) compel sympathy. In the moving scene with Miriam (p. 338) he is forced to recognize that words, even when used by one whose trade is words, may divide rather than communicate: "Miriam . . . I never say the things I mean to say! They seem to . . . turn on me . . .". And the pathos of this isolation is reinforced by the still more moving scene between Sword and Stella, the nurse whose simplicity and honesty offset the destructive pride of the Swords, who, less educated, is able to communicate more by silence than they with all their words. It is a scene to awaken the sharpest apprehension, since it could so easily topple over into sentimentality. White in fact brings it off beautifully: the dialogue is restrained yet pregnant with feeling, suggesting far more than it states, an effect that is possible in naturalistic dialogue when, and only when, the preceding scenes have generated a store of subliminal passion.

The play is not all on this level, however. Miriam never does quite convince. It may be natural for a professor's tipsy wife to call him "You . . . *intellectual!*" as the dirtiest insult she can think of, but when she also spits at him one wonders if she has strayed in from the world of *The Rose Tattoo*. And the very scene I have just praised ends with Sword's insinuation that Stella's love for her father is incestuous, which leads to her suicide and in doing so produces the effect of a contrived catastrophe. Stella's death is adequately prepared for (hints are carefully planted in her conversation with Miss Quodling in the opening scene), but the incest motif is not. It has no organic relation to the central problem, and though it provides an effective theatrical climax when it is uncertain whether it is Miriam or Stella who had disappeared over the cliff, in so far as Stella's suicide is used to convict the Swords any suggestion of factitiousness may seem to invalidate the theme.

In fact, Miss Quodling's warning that "somebody's gunna cut inter *you*" (p. 275) is fulfilled before Stella's death by the way in which both the Swords clutch at her for life and renewal. Stella belongs to "the burnt ones"—but so, too, do the Swords, though they are their own tormentors, and ultimately, perhaps, their suffering—his, at any rate—has more reality than the more phrenetic self-tortures of Albee's George and Martha. Albee, of course, has no equivalent to Miss Quodling's goat-song, through which White opposes to his world of barren, frustrated humans the world of natural fertility. It is a rather terrifying philosophy that is suggested by Miss Quodling— "In the end, you can't trust anythun but goats and silence" (p. 272)—so it is not surprising when she admits "I don't go nap on the human beings." She can "Wonder if there's any life inside of a rock . . . For all we know . . . waitun to be hurt . . . like anythink else . . ." (p. 281) without applying this to humanity. Moreover, "she never went nap on the bucks" (p. 281); she has attained her peace, her understanding of the silence of rocks, by renouncing not only human society in general but sexuality in particular, except in so far as she takes a vicarious interest in that of her goats. In the end she admits that she has run away from life: and she has to face the fact that goats too are mortal. But although she concedes Sword's point that "we're not . . . just . . . animals!" her comment "And kill ourselves because of it" (p. 352) sums up the burden of the play, another version of the theme that "the intellect has failed us". Sword's self-accusing remark to Miriam: "Even scorpions love each other after their fashion" (p. 338) is a bitter indictment of the use which humanity has made of its intelligence: the play would be Swiftian in its misanthropy if Stella were not there to provide a human alternative to the goats. But she *is* there, and the dramatist has brought off the difficult task of making her attractive in her simplicity.

If Patrick White does continue to write for the theatre there will doubtless be pressures on him to compromise (some critics betray a pathetic yearning to discover that he is one of the boys after all). It is to be hoped that he will leave to lesser talents the lesser tasks and will go on to assault peaks in drama comparable to those he has conquered in the novel. These would not, of course, exclude comedy: who more capable of giving us a modern counterpart to the elegant, civilized comedy of Congreve, with characters like Mrs Chalmers-Robinson and Mrs Furlow in place of Lady Wishfort, Lady Plyant and the rest? But, above all, one hopes for a new play in which he will scale at least the foothills leading to the *Lear* range.

4/1965

The Short Stories of Patrick White[1]

J. F. BURROWS

In one of the slightest stories in *The Burnt Ones*, there are glimpses of all the rest. "Willy-Wagtails by Moonlight" concerns a tape-recording of birdsong, in the middle of which the willy-wagtails give place to a love-scene between a married man and his secretary. No one knows of this interpolation until a couple named Wheeler, visiting the unfaithful husband and his devoted wife, are left listening to the tape. At first maliciously amused and then shocked out of their amusement, the Wheelers tacitly resolve to say nothing at all. And there the story ends.

The Wheelers are stock-figures—the malicious North Shore matron and the pompous executive—presented sharply enough but without much depth. So, too, with Arch Mackenzie, the bird-watcher gone astray, and his secretary, Miss Cullen. The real possibilities and the eventual failure of the story have to do with Nora Mackenzie.

The most obvious of Nora's three faces is that of a discreetly status-seeking hypocrite, hardly less an object of satire than her husband and her so-called friends. Her house is "what is known as a Lovely Old Home—colonial style—amongst some carefully natural-looking gums".[2] Its furnishings, insipidly ostentatious, are "period" pieces in a string-and-beige coloured setting. Despite her courses in French cookery and the like, Nora is an abominable cook, a muddling housekeeper, and an ungenerous hostess. There is even a suggestion that she became

[1] The following discussion is based on an article ("The Short Stories of Patrick White", *Southerly*, xxiv (1964), pp. 116-25) which appeared before White's stories were collected in *The Burnt Ones*. The publication of later stories, the comments of the reviewers, and a closer acquaintance with White's novels have led me to make certain revisions.

[2] *The Burnt Ones* (London, Eyre and Spottiswoode, 1964), p. 76. All references are to this edition.

a bird-watcher only in pursuit of bigger (if not nobler) game. Such a Nora would have served well in a story, after de Maupassant, of the biter bit. But this Nora is contradicted almost out of existence by other aspects of her behaviour. (It is not possible to argue that all this is only Eileen Wheeler's malicious account of Nora: the hypothesis about her bird-watching may be Eileen's; but most of Nora's other unpleasantness is remarked by an omniscient narrator.)

The second Nora is a Freudian figure whose single dominant motive is a frustrated urge for motherhood. Her spinsterish self-consciousness, her motherly devotion to Arch, her altruistic concern for his employees, even Miss Cullen, and her passionate absorption in bird-watching ("The children she had never had . . . ", p. 83) are all advanced as sublimations of the one central drive. The alliance of husband, employee, and even birds in her betrayal, the hints that she is half-conscious of Arch's infidelity, and the way in which, even when the story ends, her betrayal has yet to reach daylight, all serve to give this version a somewhat Chekhovian air. Of the three stories that are here confused, this one is not only the most fully evolved but also the most in keeping with the notion of "the burnt ones (the poor unfortunates)" (p. 5). If it were not for the distractions of its competitors, especially the former, it would make its comic-pathetic point very effectively.

The third Nora appears only briefly and is, therefore, a threat to the integrity of her sisters rather than a figure in her own right. Yet even though, in the glimpses we are given, she is blurred by self-pity, she is recognizable as a member of that little band of renegade individuals, aloof from and invulnerable to the assaults of their society, who dominate some of the other stories. In her imagination,

. . . Nora Mackenzie was standing alone amongst the inexorable moonlit gums. She thought perhaps she had always felt alone, even with Arch, while grateful even for her loneliness. (p. 87)

The clashes between these different aspects of the story emerge clearly from an examination of any of a number of passages. Thus:

Nora said they'd be more comfortable drinking their coffee in the lounge.

Then Arch fetched the tape recorder. He set it up on the Queen Anne walnut piecrust. It certainly was an impressive machine. (pp. 82-3)

Presumably this passage is ironical and not mere reportage. If so, the most obvious irony seems to be directed at those (the Wheelers?) whose shoddy "modern" values lead them to be more impressed by a tape-recorder than by such a table as this. But then, we wonder, just what sort of table *is* this? Nothing else in the Mackenzies' home suggests that their table would be "Queen Anne" in any very strict sense. If it is so only in the loose sense in which the term is used by Vulgar Australians, then presumably Nora's values as well as (or rather than?) the Wheelers' are White's target of the moment.[3] Again, we are left in doubt whether Arch's treatment of the table is to be seen as mere vandalism or as an expression of a superbly natural ability to *use* an object, whatever its snob-value, for an immediate purpose. Even the innocent-looking first sentence raises a further problem. Is it offered as the casual and sensible remark of any hostess? Or as the satiric rendering of a cliché, directed at Nora and given force by the word "lounge", a common Australianism which, by the English standards elsewhere adopted by White,[4] is distinctly non-U when it is used at all? Questions like these ought, of course, to be answerable from the text itself. But they are not—because White's satiric focus is blurred.

The kind of social satire which depends upon the registering of a multitude of socio-aesthetic signs or "manners" and which dominates the first of "my" versions of "Willy-Wagtails by Moonlight" persists, in one form or another, in all the other stories. It is at its most direct in "Miss Slattery and her Demon Lover", an uproarious farce which consists essentially in a clash of socio-sexual values between migrant male and Australian female.

When Miss Slattery, a "market researcher", encounters Tibor Szabo, a wealthy Hungarian migrant, she is almost in-

---

[3] These uncertainties are not relieved by the circumstance that the "piecrust" style post-dates the death of Queen Anne. If this contradiction is deliberate, White's satiric point recedes into an even wider landscape of possibilities.

[4] For less ambiguous examples of White's satiric use of "lounge", see *The Burnt Ones*, p. 38, and *Riders in the Chariot*, p. 330.

stantaneously seduced. For a time she remains alike overwhelmed by his lavish supply of imported *objets de bourgeois* —a Jaguar car, a mink bedspread, and so forth—and by his bland assumption that she, being Australian, exists only for him to exploit. On his side, a complacent acceptance of her physical charms overrules a profound contempt for her inertness and conventionality, especially on the subject of Love. Then, at a party, she begins cracking a stock-whip, arousing nostalgic memories in them both: in her, of an older Australia of dust, cattle, and sweaty leather; in him, of the masochistic delights of being flogged. Thereafter he finds her unique and indispensable while she, nostalgic only for a moment and bored from the first by this strange new sport, gains a complete ascendancy. He has been assimilated by a vast inertness, much as a sleepy leviathan might engulf a lonely shrimp or as Sarsaparilla seeks to engulf the Charioteers. This is not to suggest that, on his side, Tibby is even remotely like the Charioteers. As Mr Andrew Taylor puts it, in a perceptive review, Tibby is not even a "burnt one" but rather "comes in for a little humorous roasting".[5]

At the level of farce the story is admirably sustained. The clash of opposing manners is central and lucid and the manners themselves are registered with all White's verbal wit. Unfortunately, however, he is content to record manners rather than look deeply into the attitudes that manners signify.

And yet this sacrifice of depth may not be altogether a loss. Unlike the greatest writers of short stories, White usually needs ample room in which to conduct any very searching inquiry. In its portrayal of the quasi-lesbian relationship between the first Mrs Philippides and Aglaia, her servant and successor, "A Glass of Tea" is one of the subtlest and most delicately-poised of all these stories. Yet it fails through attempting too much. Mrs Philippides is never presented directly but is seen through the eyes of her widowed husband and through the imaginings of a visitor to whom, years afterwards, the old man is telling of his marriage. Even though Aglaia herself is given a few words at the end, one never knows enough of the Philippides to be sure that the husband

---

[5] "White's Short Stories", *Overland*, 31 (1965), p. 18.

is indeed a courteously complacent recipient of devotion, that the wife's devotion was long-suffering and genuine, and that her life was destroyed by her neurotic concern for and attempt to frustrate a gipsy's prophecy. Nor, again, can one be quite certain how much of all this is the work of the visitor's fertile imagination. In this story White is working in a mode akin to that of Part Two of *The Aunt's Story* but, for want of a Part One, he never attains the sure ground of that novel.

A second group of stories, making up the bulk of the collection, is concerned with frustrations and sublimations akin to those of the second Nora Mackenzie. Widely as they differ in appearance, three of them—"The Letters", "Clay", and "Being Kind to Titina"—are virtually text-book instances of one or another of the classic manifestations of the Oedipus complex. There are Oedipal moments in other stories—notably "The Evening at Sissy Kamara's", "A Glass of Tea", "Dead Roses", and "The Woman who wasn't Allowed to Keep Cats"; but, in these others, the traumatic experience from which the sufferings of the "burnt one" really stem is an experience of adolescence or maturity rather than one of infancy. In all of these Freudian stories, the broader social setting, though at times seriously obtrusive, is essentially incidental.

"The Letters", where an adult son fears for a moment that his eyes will be gouged out by his mother's brooch, shows the Oedipal pattern at its simplest. Mrs Polkinghorn babies Charles all his life ("Sometimes the mother almost expected to see a pulse still beating in her child's head", p. 226). On his fiftieth birthday, suddenly deprived of the aunt in whom he had found an unaggressive mother-substitute, he betters his mother's instruction by assaulting her in an attempt at suckling. The setting, like his mistress, is Sarsaparilla-Olde-Englyshe, and it provides the occasion for touches of satire which are neat enough in themselves but which lack any very fully-imagined connection with the central action. The one moment of real poignancy comes when, from the depths of Charles's memories of the university which had been his one and Elyot Standish-like hope of escape, there floats up as unidentified but painfully relevant French tag. It is a line from Racine, spoken when Phèdre is about to explode into confessing her love for Hippolyte: "De l'amour j'ai toutes les fureurs."

In "Clay" a feeble but "poetic" son is driven from a mother whom he loves and hates, both passionately, to a wife who is her replica in everyday behaviour but whose emotional life hardly exists. His dreams of freedom from his mother's tyranny turn, after her death, to grotesquely comic orgies of imagined incest. The mother-figure of these affairs, whom he calls Lova, bedevils him increasingly until the story ends in a manner no less erotic but mercifully less earnest than the ending of "The Letters".

The other major variant of Freud's mother-son relationship gives point to "Being Kind to Titina". Here a Graeco-Alexandrian youth of the present day is so fortunate as to experience in real life what amounts to an erotic daydream of Ceres in all her bounty. This nervous youth (whose name is Dionysios) is showered with maternal gold, culminating in a gentle and expert induction in the art of love. The story varies the text-book formula in another way also: for Titina, the serene patroness, is not the boy's mother at all but a little whore, younger than himself, whose patron *he* had been in their childhood. This oddly pleasant and amusing tale is marred by a sudden and forced attempt to turn Dionysios from an ordinarily diffident youth into a "burnt one", betrayed by mother-substitute as well as mother ("I realized that my extended throat was itself a stiff sword", p. 205).

Notwithstanding their incidental merits, these three stories are damaged by the mechanical working-out of a pre-ordained idea. Apart from those gestures which are designed as Oedipal symbols, the "manners" of these stories are, on the whole, neither closely observed nor very rich in meanings.

Of the four Freudian stories which are not primarily Oedipal, "A Glass of Tea" has already been touched on. In "The Evening at Sissy Kamara's", White rather crudely attempts to set his long-standing concern with the nature of suffering in a new perspective.

As her dentist sets about drilling a rotten tooth, the thoughts of Mrs Poppy Pantzopoulos range widely, though less irrelevantly than she supposes. There is, nearest at hand, a pompous conviction that it is "her duty to test her capacity for suffering" (p. 134). There is a strong awareness of the dentist as a quasi-sexual aggressor, a point that White makes through his habitual emphasis on hairiness and also through a blatant symbolism:

> Now she watched, with fascinated langour, from beneath her eyelids, the dentist's strong and hairy wrists, as he stooped, and breathed, and prepared the drill. ...
> Then Mr Petrocheilos was opening her mouth as though it were a rubber slit. He was inserting an enormous finger. He was introducing the dreadful drill. ...
> Mr Petrocheilos breathed fire into Mrs Pantzopoulos' face. The caverns of black, wiry hair threatened to engulf. (pp. 134-35)

There is, again, a drifting into recollections of "incidents of no significance. For example, the evening at Sissy Kamara's" (p. 134).

From these "insignificant" recollections, it emerges that Mrs Pantzopoulos, devoted as she is to the theory of suffering, is insensitive to almost anything but physical pain. She has knowingly submitted to being married, simply for her money, by an egocentric social climber. She can hardly be blamed for submitting to his contemptuous amusement at Sissy Kamara, a ludicrous blue-stocking who had been her childhood friend in Smyrna. Her willingness to join her husband in scorning Sissy's husband is another matter: for, as she is aware, the ineffectual Sotos Louloudis is genuinely sensitive, humble, and long-suffering.

When the dentist's drill penetrates to the nerve of her tooth, the association of her immediate pain and her interrupted thoughts of the evening at Sissy Kamara's gives rise to a sudden and overpowering recollection of an incident she has long repressed. For, on that evening, she had been reminded of Vangelio, an old maid-servant who had been Sissy's nurse and an admirer of her own. Fleeing towards the Quay from the burning town of Smyrna,[6] as she only now remem-

---

[6] The terrible events in Smyrna during the period 1919-22 figure also, though less centrally, in "A Glass of Tea" and "Being Kind to Titina". A lucid account of the whole matter is given by G. M. Gathorne-Hardy, *A Short History of International Affairs: 1920-39*, O.U.P. (1934: 4th edn., 1950), pp. 115-22.

bers, she had seen Vangelio being stabbed to death by a Turk. Her emotional anaesthesia, we are given to understand, began in her repression of this incident and has accordingly consisted, above all, in a fear of any kind of "stabbing". Thus reminded of that bygone moment, she faces it squarely, accepting that one must not seek to insulate oneself from Life. Through a renewed ability to suffer, she recovers her capacity for living.

Although one would wish to make every allowance for the strait limits of the short story as a literary form, the subtle and fully-absorbed Freudianism of White's novels makes it difficult to take this story seriously. The symbolism is blatant throughout; the sack of Smyrna loses emotional force through an overinsistent technique ("What can one do running jumping faces? Seize the knife the flesh parting bone wincing? Oh no, not that! Or would it have hurt less than the omission?", p. 149); and the climatic, all-healing moment of self-knowledge takes the form of an offer to pay the dentist at once lest she be killed by a bus while crossing the square. Such merits as the story has are at its fringes, as in its satirical strokes at the expense of the abominable Basil Pantzopoulos: "Basil touched his black pearl, the one he always wore in his tie. He had grown so flawless he could afford to forget his original grain of Piraeus sand." (p. 135)

A grave unevenness of tone in "The Woman who wasn't Allowed to Keep Cats" faces the critic with tricky problems of emphasis. In the article on which this discussion is based, I spoke of this story as "a rambling and portentous tale of lesbians, marital troubles, and cat-worship, too much of which is given over to cheap contrasts between Greek Greeks and Americanized Greeks" (*op. cit.*, 120). In his review of *The Burnt Ones*, on the other hand, Mr Andrew Taylor sees more deeply:

... the main contrast in one of the best stories ... is not between the Greeks and their Americanized visitors, but between an indulgent and smothering sensuality that bores, tires, or irritates, and the sharp feline sexuality that succeeds it. (*op. cit.*, 18)

In the central action of the story, where Mr Taylor's emphasis falls, the career of Kikitsa Alexiou is indeed predominantly feline. Her lesbian seduction, in their youth, of Maro

Hajistavros had been less that of person by person than of cat by cat:

> After that Kikitsa did something so extraordinary it was difficult to recall in detail, only as a scurry of bronze, of furred light, and the crackle of dried heather twigs.
> 'See?' Kikitsa breathed as soon as she had withdrawn. 'A little, thin, cat's tongue!'
> Maro's mouth had melted for a moment in the sun.
> 'And you, *chrysoula*,' murmured Kikitsa through her teeth, 'are a kind of little, thin cat.' (p. 273)

Afterwards, as victim of an unfulfilling marriage to a pretentious, self-absorbed, and sleepy *littérateur*, Kikitsa sublimates her sexuality in a sluttishly comatose devotion to a tribe of actual cats whom she encourages to overrun her house. When Aleko Alexiou unexpectedly succeeds as a writer, his new-found self-respect enables him to dismiss the cats and to set about meeting his wife's needs. Since Kikitsa is inescapably feline by now, his wooing is cat-like:

> Was it the Kyria Alexiou, then, who suddenly sprang on the stump of one of the martyred trees? Her teeth glittered in the moonlight.
> Long, long moments, passed.
> Then it was the Kyrios Alexiou who sprang. The scents, the cold draughts of air were quite intoxicating. The Kyrios sprang as though he had been wound up for it. How his trouser-legs streamed black in his wake. As the Kyria Kikitsa leaped away, as white by moonlight as the stump from which the resin had run, Anthoula did not exactly see, but knew he had fastened his teeth in the nape of the white neck.
> Beyond, where the moonlight was dappled with darkness, all was a wrestling of light with dark.
> Did Kyria Alexiou shriek?
> Kyria Photini began to pant.
> 'Did you see? Did you hear, Anthoula? What is happening?' . . . Anthoula laughed and laughed.
> 'Some people,' she said, more for herself than her companion, 'some people find the cat that suits them.' (pp. 279-80)

Meanwhile Maro has long since completely repressed the lesbian incident, fled to America, and married an only too Sarsaparillan fellow-migrant. When they revisit Greece, she is as last obliged to remember that moment. Unable, however, to face the memory, she retreats from Life once more:

> ... she would not, would not allow herself to disintegrate. She closed her eyes against present and past. How glad she was, really, to be in a position to look forward to America. Even the distress of the Atlantic flight, the constriction, anxiety, the pills which would not work, struck her as desirable, and to walk at last inside their own apartment door, to discover whether she had been dreaming, or whether her india-rubber tree had died. (p. 282)

Especially where Kikitsa is concerned, the story has many moments of real strength. And even Maro's continuance in her neurosis is more convincingly rendered than Poppy Pantzo-poulos's miraculous recovery from hers. To concede all this, however, is not to give up my original contention that too much of the story is given over to cheap contrasts, through which its centre is obscured and in which an uncontrolled wit undermines the sympathy that the story asks of us. Although White's sub-olympian detachment from his characters generally might find defenders, it is the slovenly Kikitsa of the lines following whom we are asked to accept—after a change of heart and a slimming-course—as the feline love-dancer of the second passage quoted:

> ... when they had left the car, and climbed with grudging, almost fearful steps upon what remained of the little temple, Kikitsa asked a vaster audience:
> 'What do you say if I dance?'
> It was not surprising nobody answered, though Maro was surprised and grateful that, despite discouragement, her friend did not choose to begin. Instead, she flopped down. Against a column. A fat woman, in middle age, and a mackintosh with a grease-mark on it. (p. 261)

"Dead Roses", much the longest of White's stories, is prettily summed up by Dr Heseltine as "a blueprint of how Anthea Scudamore turns into her mother".[7] The change in Anthea follows familiar lines. As a girl she is dominated by a mother as genteelly cannibalistic as any in White's work, and finds her-

---

[7] H. P. Heseltine, in a review of *The Burnt Ones*, *Southerly*, XXV (1965), p. 71.

self cut off from her decent but defeated father. If her parents are a reincarnation of George and Julia Goodman, the young Anthea is no Theodora. As the story opens, at a time when the amiable Tullochs—a couple whose complacency is mocked far more gently than is usual in *The Burnt Ones*—invite her to spend a holiday at their beach-house, Anthea is clay in the hands of whatever potter she may chance to meet.

The Tullochs have brought her there in the hope of " 'giving her a push in what her mother will consider the wrong direction' " (p. 12). Unfortunately for Anthea, Barry Flegg, the young man they set to work on her, is too heavy-handed altogether. During the weeks of her stay with the Tullochs, she finds herself increasingly, though timorously, responsive to his overtures, and increasingly resistant to her mother's nightly phone-calls. At the crucial moment, however, he is too sudden and too violent. It is her mother's girl who, overcome with relief that, after all, he had "respected her distress" (p. 28), comments sententiously:

> 'I'd always hoped,' she said, 'I'd fall in love.'
> 'Why not?' he replied, looking at her without resentment. 'That's what we're all trying for. But have to learn it.'
> 'Not like animals.'
> 'We are, aren't we? With instincts for decency thrown in.'
> She preferred to nurse, not so much her bruised sides, as a moral injury she might have enjoyed sustaining.
> 'It's not the way I look at it,' she said. 'It's more,' she said, 'something finer.' (pp. 28-9)

Anthea hastily retreats into her mother's arms and, no time afterwards, into marriage to the elderly and impotent Hessell Mortlock, a wealthy visitor from Sarsaparilla. To more observant eyes than those of mother and daughter, there are warnings from the first that Mortlock is not what he seems. His splendid gift of roses, for example, comes at a time when they are a glut on the market. With more room to move than in the other stories, White gives such *motifs* a genuine association with these particular characters. Perhaps for the same reason, his account of the marriage is perceptive in its compassion as well as its severity. Gradually Anthea moves from a rather respectful fondness for her "Daddy", as she once calls him (p. 51), to detestation of his ingenious miserliness, frustration at his impotence, and disgust for his well-preserved public face.

At last, after more than ten years, she leaves him. Through the accident of his dying before he can disinherit her, she is left a wealthy widow. Like the dreams of Barry Flegg that had punctuated her married life, her unaccompanied stay at the Tullochs' beach-house is a natural and, as it proves, subtle expression of what she has become:

> She clumped like an animal through the scrub. Or stalked birdlike over the sand. So deserted was her desert beach that she took off her clothes once, without even looking over her shoulder, and walked into the milky sea. Exquisite skirts of foam clung to her ankles, and began to soothe her thighs. It was so gently perfect in the healing water that she closed her eyes and almost understood which direction was the right one. But it floated out of her grasp, together with the capsules of weed, as though almost is the most.
>
> At least she did not expect complete enlightenment, and rose, content enough to re-enter the solid sculpture of her body. To put on the clothes she found. To notice the remote rocks which hid the wrestling-match of her girlhood. What she had regarded then as ugly, monstrous, frightening, she now saw as merely undesirable, or absurd. And went away along the hard sand, thoughtfully combing out her hair with her fingers, to let it dry.
>
> Absurd. Yes, absurd. That night Mrs Mortlock realized her condition was easily curable. (pp. 64-65)

This easy "cure" is, of course, to close her eyes. By now she is indeed her mother. After this, the last episode is as unnecessary as it is contrived. She goes abroad and, by the *merest* chance, meets Barry Flegg complete with healthy, natural family. When he tosses his wife a bunch of roses, she offers them to Anthea:

> 'Oh no! Please!' Mrs Mortlock protested.
> Her lips were trembling unaccountably under the last flakes of lipstick.
> 'Or perhaps one,' she begged.
> And pinned the rose with a brooch, which seemed, rather, to draw attention to the diamonds, though she had not intended it that way.

'Flowers die on me,' she apologized, 'very quickly.'

She spoke more softly than was her habit, almost childlike, while glancing sideways at Mrs Flegg, who continued sitting for a moment abandoned in time, it might have appeared, but for the evidence of children, and the crimson roses, glowing and spilling from her stained lap. (p. 72)

As she leaves the Fleggs to walk back to her hotel, she becomes convinced that a man is chasing her. Although it is her own unruly imagination from which she is really fleeing she does, for the moment, find security in her hotel room and a volume of Frances Parkinson Keyes.

The many fine things in "Dead Roses" lose some of their effect because of one's sense of having been there before. White's long-standing preoccupation with suffering will hardly leave him now; and it may well be that, within this particular labyrinth of the imagination, unknown passages will yet open before him and amply repay the exploring. But little remains within reach of the brief and lightly-equipped excursions of these Freudian stories. Comic or serious, Oedipal or adult, illuminated or for ever dark, the passages through which the "burnt ones" stumble are known to White stone by symbolic stone.

The fact that the Greek stories all fall into this Freudian group coupled with the fact that the two remaining stories, which do not, are Sarsaparillan makes it plain that it is not Sarsaparilla as such that White has exhausted. These last two stories, "A Cheery Soul" and "Down at the Dump", deal not with "burnt ones" but with successful renegades of the kind foreshadowed by the third Nora Mackenzie. Yet they differ as widely from each other as from the rest.

By way of background to them, let us sum up the social setting of the other stories. There are many moments of acute and penetrating observation and some sustained but rather limited conflicts of manners. There are, on the other hand, occasions when, as *Riders in the Chariot* would lead us to expect, Sarsaparilla becomes a distracting stage-villain. On such occasions, the Mackenzies' "carefully natural-looking gums" (p. 76), Hessell Mortlock's roses and photinias, Mrs Polkinghorn's exotic shrubs, and the "bald, red, rudimentary hill" (*Riders in the Chariot*, p. 545), clad only in Iceland poppies and gladioli, to which Xanadu is reduced all stand as signs of the one Australian Ugliness. On such occasions a term so vague and all-embracing as "plastic"[8] comes to be used by a serious writer as an adequate symbol for what he finds wrong with our society. And on such occasions even chastity is seen as mere subservience to convention.

The force of these strictures is admirably borne out, by sheer contrast, in "A Cheery Soul",[9] to which none of them has any serious application. It is as if Mr White awoke one morning and saw his world with fresh eyes. In this story alone he sees virtue in Sarsaparilla's mustering of its forces against a rebellious individual. Yet this is no mere reversal: appalling as she is, Miss Docker has her side of the argument and must share in the pity that we more willingly bestow on her victims. And yet, again, her individuality lies in the nature of her tyranny, for, absolutely convinced of her own wisdom, she sins by an iron benevolence. Her victims know, as Charles Dickens never learnt, what it is to be at the mercy of John Jarndyce.

Of her earlier life we are told little except that, like any other cuckoo-chicken, she has had to fend for herself since infancy. Her amiable confidence that other people are merely replicas of herself and that, being imperfect replicas, their vocation is to serve her has the air of something congenital, something confirmed rather than created when she learns of Manon Lescaut. Sharing Manon's attitudes but lacking her particular gifts, Miss Docker has to seek a little further for her one unique vocation. The revelation comes finally from the natural source of revelations:

'I once read the Bible from cover to cover. That was when I was at the end of me tether. A whole fortnight it took me. I lay in bed, and read, and read. It was raining cats and dogs. Never stopped. Before that I was a pagan. But suddenly I saw.'

'What did you see?'

Ted Custance was looking at her now.

[8] The comparative infrequency of the word in *The Burnt Ones* suggests that White is learning to live with, if not to love, the "plastic" that formerly obsessed him.

[9] In "Patrick White's Four Plays", *Australian Literary Studies*, ii (1966), 155-70, I have touched on the relationships between this story and the play of the same name.

'Don't be silly!' she said. 'You can't say what you see. But *see*!' (p. 158)

Even though she cannot say what she saw, there is no doubt at all that Miss Docker saw it. And we come to see it, too. It is the simple but magnificent notion of employing Christian attitudes, such as truthfulness, charity and loving-kindness, as weapons in her fight with a society whose lip-service to Christianity renders it completely vulnerable to her. Even when, as in the rector, she assails a more genuine faith, her self-confidence quite outmatches his humility:

'If you really *insist* on cutting the grass,' the rector said as usual, 'I shall go inside and compose my sermon.'
Then Miss Docker did something awful, she could not resist. She was pushing the push-mower all the while, clatter and slash, as if to reduce an enormity. Not that truth must ever be reduced. Her misfortune, she knew, was that always, always, she had to introduce the naked truth.
'I can only be frank,' Miss Docker admitted. 'The trouble with you,' she said, 'Mr Wakeman, and a serious one in a clergyman' —all the time clatter and slash—'you cannot seem to learn to preach.'
The rector was too large to stun. But he stood there holding his buttocks, his jaws working on unformed words, or suspicion confirmed.
'Somehow you do not give yourself to it,' Miss Docker pursued, crunching with her foot.
Then Mr Wakeman turned very dark for a blond man. He said:
'I cannot argue with you, Miss Docker, on that point. Naturally, you must be the best judge.'
'I see that I have touched you on a raw nerve, and am sorry for it,' Miss Docker replied.
She had run the mower all along the border. The rector followed out of sense of duty.
'On the contrary,' he said. 'I am open to criticism. In every way. Otherwise, I should scarcely be fit to serve Our Lord.' (p. 179)

Since she is neither superficial nor inconsistent in her attitudes, she is able to win from the halt and lame the upkeep and the gratitude that are her chief social satisfactions. Since it is her specialty to act as unpaid nurse-housekeeper in households where the husband is weak or ailing, she is able to gain vicarious sexual satisfactions. And since she is no mere hypocrite, but a person absolutely self-persuaded, she is even able to solace her soul.

When she meets resistance and "ingratitude", Miss Docker pityingly but bravely moves elsewhere. At last she overreaches herself. Even so, society's victory comes less through direct resistance than through a tacit conspiracy to ignore, even to deny, her existence. Thus an old people's home rapidly depopulates itself and the congregation of the local church disappears almost overnight. One sees their point. And yet, as she trudges along the empty street at the end, one neither fully believes nor even wholly wishes her downfall to be permanent.

As a natural consequence of this awareness that, even in Sarsaparilla, society is made up of people and that a Rebellious Individual is not necessarily admirable, White's portrayal of manners takes on, almost without exception, a depth and subtlety that are lacking elsewhere. Whether she is begging the shrewdly obstinate Ted Custance to use her Christian name, plastering a woman newly-widowed with lipstick, entertaining old people with photographs of herself, or choosing the hymns that she, as sole survivor of the choir, will sing, Miss Docker is unique. And the Sarsaparillans who are her victims are observed in a spirit of gentle mockery:

    That evening Mrs Custance decided to tell her husband they must do something about Miss Docker.
    '*That* old ratbag,' Ted Custance began.
    'She is such a cheery soul,' his wife hurried, over-bright. 'Always so helpful. Doing for others what is never done for her.'
    Ted Custance, who was finishing his thirtieth summer with the bank, could not have felt gloomier. . . .
    'And what do you propose to do?' asked Mr Custance, when it seemed he must surrender.
    Mrs Custance watched her own hands cutting a piece of recalcitrant crust.
    'Well,' she said, 'I will tell you. What I would like to do is to ask Miss Docker to accept'—she chose the word with particular care—'to come and live in our little glassed-in veranda-room. She could repay us by helping with the chores. Not *rigidly*,' she hastened to add. 'I would not make a slave of anyone. Otherwise

she would be quite free. And is in such demand. She is always hemming and mending, and sitting with the old or young. We shall hardly notice she is here.'

Ted Custance freed his teeth. It had to be admitted he was not so well acquainted with Miss Docker. He was a silent, grizzled man, above all suspicious of the human animal.

'No one else in Sarsaparilla,' Mrs Custance continued to persuade, 'can equal Miss Docker at doing good.'

Mr Custance made a tired noise through his moustache.

'Provided it is not you,' he said, 'who are having a fly at doing good, I shall not worry all that much.' (pp. 151-52)

If the loving-kindness of Mrs Godbold, White's other main purveyor of that commodity, is overstrained not only by the way in which the woman herself is presented but also by White's doctrinaire insistence on the worthlessness of most of its recipients, that of Miss Docker is a quite spontaneous overflow of powerful feelings on her part springing from a rare tranquillity in White himself.

Daise Morrow, the chief social renegade of "Down at the Dump"[10], has lately died and those Sarsaparillans who must are attending her funeral. Since her rebellion had consisted in a warm-hearted and predominantly sexual love for her fellows, which the more prurient characters regard as nymphomania, the tone of the story is mainly reminiscent. All the obvious attitudes are represented, from the envious frustration of her brother-in-law to the pathetic gratitude of her last lover, from the puritanical intolerance of her sister to the promise of reincarnation in the sister's daughter. The schematic quality of the story is most apparent in the threefold contrast between Daise herself, her sister, and the lustful Mum Whalley. If what we learn of Daise's life represents a valid mediation between these extremes, there is still too much of Mrs Godbold in her ghostly "song" of praise and affirmation:

> Truly, we needn't experience tortures, unless we build chambers in our minds to house instruments of hatred in. Don't you know, my darling creatures, that death isn't death, unless it's the death of love? Love should be the greatest explosion it is reason-

---

[10] I am indebted to Dr Heseltine's review for an enhanced understanding of this story.

able to expect. Which sends us whirling, spinning, creating millions of other worlds. Never destroying. (pp. 309-10)

The conventional Sarsaparillans like Mrs Hogben, the sister, are as conventional as ever and as contemptuously treated. Yet it is encouraging to find, in the person of Mum Whalley, that White has at last come to set Mrs Lusty in a context where he can condemn her without feeling that he is denying Life. Far more important, however, are the adolescents, Meg Hogben and Lum Whalley: for in them White sees that Sarsaparilla can be transcended rather than dismissed out of hand.

Meg is the less original conception. At first she merely rejects the things her mother cherishes:

They were going out through the fuchsia bushes, past the plaster pixies, which Mrs Hogben had trained her child to cover with plastic at the first drops of rain. Meg Hogben hated the sight of those corny old pixies, even after the plastic cones had snuffed them out. (pp. 292-93)

But, as they drive past Daise's house on the way to the funeral, she begins to discover something more positive and more genuinely her own to replace the pixies:

How the mornings used to sparkle in which Aunt Daise went up and down between the rows, her gown dragging heavy with dew, binding with bast the fuzzy flowers by handfuls and handfuls. Auntie's voice clear as morning. No one, she called, could argue they look stiff when they're bunched tight eh Meg what would you say they remind you of? But you never knew the answers to the sort of things people asked. Frozen fireworks, Daise suggested. Meg loved the idea of it, she loved Daise. Not so frozen either, she dared. The sun getting at the wet flowers broke them up and made them spin.

And the clovey scent rose up in the stale-smelling car, and smote Meg Hogben, out of the reeling heads of flowers, their cold stalks dusted with blue. Then she knew she would write a poem about Aunt Daise and the carnations. She wondered she hadn't thought of it before. (p. 293)

Already she has a firmer basis for her poem than had the grandson of *The Tree of Man* and a less sexually-governed understanding of things than young Pippy had in *The Season at Sarsaparilla*.

Escaping from the funeral-party, Meg wanders through the rubbish-dump that adjoins the cemetery until she meets Lum Whalley, of whom she has always been a little afraid. As they walk together, each shyly gives expression to an adolescent sexuality which reaches a delicate culmination when "fright and expectation melted their mouths. And they took little grateful sips of each other. Holding up their throats in between. Like birds drinking." (p. 307)

But White subtly qualifies what seems all too familiar an outcome. While they were talking, Meg had responded powerfully to an aspect of Lum Whalley which represents a quite new direction for his creator. And, after Mrs Hogben discovers them kissing, Meg defends her new conception of things not by romanticizing Lum as her only playboy but by a renewed determination to resist her mother's prejudices and to find her own path.

Lum, too, is intent on finding a path of his own: "He had had about enough of this rubbish jazz. He would have liked to know how to live neat. Like Darkie Black. Everything in its place in the cabin of Darkie's trailer. Suddenly his throat yearned for Darkie's company. Darkie's hands, twisting the wheel, appeared to control the whole world" (p. 295). When Meg persuades him to tell her of these ambitions, he is as inarticulate but genuine as Stan Parker. And, if his "choice of life" seems less attractive than the traditional rustic pieties, it is, in our society, a more valid choice than any primitivistic attempt to worship at the shrines of gods who have fled for ever.

As they talk together, they both picture Meg as the wife of a semi-trailer driver. Yet, once again, White's point is not that they will remain bound to each other by a moment of youthful sympathy but that each is capable of a sympathetic response to a fellow-creature. For, as their cars pass on the way home, they both "lowered their eyes, as if they had seen enough for the present, and wished to cherish what they knew" (p. 314).

TEN ESSAYS ON PATRICK WHITE

5.45
N/AC